THE PERFECT SETTING

The PERFECT SETTING

PERI WOLFMAN & CHARLES GOLD

HARRY N. ABRAMS, INC., PUBLISHERS, NEW YORK

*To my mother, Gertrude, my grandmother, Pauline,
and my dog, Poncho, for whom they both cooked.*

C.G.

*To my father, M.G. Levine, who taught me how to
set a table, and to my mother, Mimi, who always
dined in style.*

P.W.

PROJECT DIRECTOR • MARGARET L. KAPLAN

EDITOR • RUTH PELTASON

DESIGNER • JUDITH HENRY

Grateful acknowledgment is made to the following publishers for permission to reprint recipes:
The Soho Charcuterie Cookbook, William Morrow and Company, Inc., 1983; *The Silver Palate Cookbook*,
Workman Publishing Company, Inc., 1982; *Cosmopolitan* Magazine, © 1983 The Hearst Corporation,
for the following recipes: *Cranberry/Maple Apples, Zesty Bosc Pears, Seckel Pears
Almondine, Oranges in Port Wine.*

The photographs on pages 122 and 123 are reprinted from *Cosmopolitan* Magazine, © 1983 The Hearst Corporation.
The photograph on page 47 is reprinted from *House & Garden.* Copyright 1980 by The Condé Nast Publications Inc.
The authors wish to thank the following photographers for permission to reproduce their works:
Corrine Colen, Ken Druse, Brigitte Lacombe, Elyse Lewin, Russell MacMasters, Chris Mead.

Library of Congress Cataloging in Publication Data
Wolfman, Peri. The perfect setting.
1. Table setting and decoration. 2. Cookery.
3. Tableware—Catalogs. I. Gold, Charles. II.Title.
TX871.W65 1985   641'.6   85–3904
ISBN 0–8109–1482–4

CONTENTS

INTRODUCTION

I cannot remember the time before I enjoyed setting a pretty table.

I grew up in a suburb of New York in a modest house on a street shaded by old trees. At a time when most people around us were modernizing, and family heirlooms were becoming an anachronism, we still set our table with antique silver, cloth napkins, and wineglasses. Our most valuable possessions were also our most used. We were heirs to a set of extraordinary flatware, extraordinary not because of its monetary value, but because of its rich history. It had been handed down from my stepmother's grandparents, who had commissioned it for their hotel, The Hotel New York, in Marienbad, Czechoslovakia. My stepmother used to tell us that the silverware was used by the visiting royalty who frequented the hotel. But she also made it clear that the silverware was now at our house to be used and enjoyed.

I must have been the only seven-year-old on the block who knew what a fish fork and a fish knife were. And we were probably the only household where the father, a lawyer who loved to cook, was the family chef. My stepmother was sous-chef and in charge of cleanup. Being the eldest daughter, my job was setting the table. There were so many beautiful things that could be laid on the table in so many ways. I loved setting out the huge European dessert spoons, the perfectly round bouillon spoons, the elaborate ice cream forks, the strangely shaped butter spreader—often for purposes not originally intended.

I learned early on that setting a table is so much more than just laying down knives and forks. It is creating a setting for food and conversation, setting a mood and an aura that lingers long after what was served and who said what are forgotten.

When I think back to our family meals, it isn't the taste or smell of the food that I recall as much as the way the scene looked: the ambiance of the table, the patina of the wood, the candlelight, the colors, the sense of harmony and order.

In our house a wonderful incongruity existed between elegant heirlooms and our modest life-style. It is that same incongruity which I embrace today as the spirit and essence of any table setting. In my home today, lace napkins are on our bare pine table, heavy pottery dinner plates underneath delicate hand-painted nineteenth-century Portuguese dishes, an ornate fish fork alongside a twig basket of pastries. This is the stuff of which style is made.

And so, for me dining became an art, the idea that the ambiance of a table was central to the success of a meal. But the lasting importance of all that early childhood table setting was not immediately apparent to me. I went on to design school, originally choosing a career as a clothing designer. It was some time later, when I was married and had a house and family of my own, that I realized my real love of style was in the home.

Moving to San Francisco from New York in 1972 gave me a new perspective on style, and the opportunity to apply my designing skills to restoration, interior design, and my own home. I often entertained, enjoying the abundance of fresh foods California had to offer and the simpler approach to cooking. This abundance of produce spilled over into the setting of the table. It was natural, it seemed, to have a basket of oranges on the kitchen table, a bowl of bright green peppers on the sideboard, and two or three pitchers filled with bunches of wild flowers on the dining room table. Later, when Charley Gold and I met, I returned to New York, but the California love of things fresh and uncluttered stayed with me.

Charley had trained in ceramic design at Alfred University, where he received a master's degree in fine art. He started his career in a New York advertising agency as a photographer before opening his own studio. Still lifes and food became his specialty and cooking became his avocation, or more accurately, his passion.

When we and our combined family of four boys moved to an apartment in New York City, we decided to simplify our surroundings to contrast with the frantic pace of the city and our large, energetic family. We eliminated clutter and limited our color palette, down to, and including, our tableware. We edited the masses of stuff we had accumulated in our separate lives over the years. We chose to keep myriad shapes and sizes, but only in white because it looked so clean and pure (with the exception of Charley's natural stoneware bowls). Our kitchen completed, our chinaware edited and massed on open shelves—this was when we fell in love with the sculptural quality of the heavy white china that had been available only through distributors of hotel and restaurant tableware.

The only real color we kept was in the dozens of sets of napkins that were tucked away in drawers, awaiting their own particular turn at the table. And our only remaining clutter was a wide variety of flatware—from new plastic-handle place settings to antique English butter knives and my family's prized fish forks and fish knives. Like the napkins, these were also kept in drawers, to be taken out when needed to vary the table according to our mood, the time of day, the kind of food being served, to underline an occasion, or to spark a celebration.

When Charley and I are at home he usually cooks and I usually set the table. However, there are times when I will come home not only to a fully prepared meal but to a fully set table as well! It is fascinating to me that he can take the same elements I would have used and achieve a completely different effect. Charley always creates a more "lived-in" look with his table settings—an unfolded, draped napkin, a bandana tied around the neck of a wine bottle. I tend toward a more traditional style. In our house you can always tell who has set the table.

Our kitchen filled to capacity and our minds filled with ideas, we decided to open a store. In 1981 we opened the first Wolfman · Gold & Good Company in a beautiful, landmark building in New York's historic Soho district.

We soon discovered that what we were doing was selling a look—perhaps even a life-style—

instead of various individual dishes, pitchers, and bowls. Customers bought entire table settings we displayed. Like us, they bought dish towels to use as place mats, bandanas to use as napkins, straw cheese baskets as place mats, oversized water goblets as wineglasses. They did not want these things simply because they were practical, pretty, and affordable. They were responding to them as basic elements, simple enough to be combined with their own possessions, straightforward enough to be right in any kind of setting.

At this point we wanted to define and refine our thoughts about tables and table settings in both words and pictures. To us, the photographer and the designer, that meant a book.

As shop owners we had every resource available to us. Whether it was a picnic, a buffet, or a party, we had visions of what the perfect setting might be. But as we got to work on creating these settings for the book, we discovered that perhaps our most valuable resource was our friends. They offered assistance, and they loaned their many unique and precious objects. And most important, there were those friends who invited us over for meals, and so opened up to us a range of possibilities: from setting whimsical tables, cluttered tables, tables that made wonderful use of personal collections, and tables that truly reflected the people who set them. We broadened our horizons and have a richer story to tell as a result. More often than not, when we were invited out to dinner, away for the weekend, or even ordered a picnic-to-go, along came Charley's cameras. And so you'll find we have come up with a spectrum of settings, from breakfast alfresco to a Russian Christmas.

All of this served to confirm in us our conviction that setting the table is at least as important as cooking the food. Of course good food is important; without the food there would be no meal. But there are simply delicious foods one can buy which require little in the way of preparation or cooking skills: cheeses and pâtés, crudités, and other infinite choices at a gourmet shop. But once the table is set, so is the mood and attitude for the experience.

Happily, style no longer has anything to do with spending a great deal of money. In fact, people who are forced to use their ingenuity usually end up with better results—or more of a personal style—than those who can afford the "matched set."

Our menus today are eclectic; often we'll combine the earthy with the elegant. We enjoy truffles swirled into pasta, caviar on baked potatoes. In similar fashion, baskets look beautiful alongside antique silver, white restaurant china marries well with delicate goblets, lacy paper doilies contrast elegantly on top of a bare pine table.

Much as we love a beautiful, creative table setting, we emphatically believe that if it cannot be done between car pools, after the committee meeting is over, between the office and dinner, comfortably and easily, we just will not do it. Charley and I don't follow a recipe that takes three days of preparation, nor do we spend three hours setting the table, no matter what the end result might be. If having guests means dragging out dishes that have not been used in ages, washing and polishing things that we have not used in months, it is simply not worth it.

To be a successful table setter, try to develop an individual style by keeping your beautiful things ready to hand and in constant use. It is in the mood and spirit of these hectic times to set a beautiful table every night based on the simple, the doable, and the affordable. Not only will your family sit up straighter and speak a little more politely—you have the added benefit of knowing that if a guest drops in, you won't drop dead!

Brillat-Savarin was not only referring to the food when he said, "The pleasures of the table may be enjoyed every day, in every climate, at all ages, and by all conditions of man." It is the mood and style of the table set creatively and originally that will transform even the most ordinary fare—whether with family or friends—into a party, a delight, a joy.

PERI WOLFMAN
New York City, 1985

ELEMENTS

*T*hese are our shelves, and on them, a few of our favorite things. This chapter introduces a cast of characters that will assume many different roles in the settings that follow. We are not attempting to catalogue the broad range of tableware available today. Our purpose, instead, is to show the elements that we love and that work best for us; elements that can be used for a multitude of purposes and which are easily adaptable, alone or in combination with each other.

To begin with, we like our plates, bowls, and platters big, bold, and white. A large number of the same kind of plates and bowls look great when massed on kitchen shelves or on a buffet table; plus, when a holiday or a special occasion rolls around there are always enough dishes for a large party. Simple white tableware works with any food and shows off to great advantage colorful sauces and garnishes. It gives you free rein with the table linens, glasses, flatware, and flowers; simply put, it is a perfect backdrop for any look you care to create.

Our basic dinner plates are buffet size; they look wonderful by themselves and even better when layered with other tableware. The bowls are big enough to twirl pasta without spilling the sauce, hold a double portion of salad, or a main course of soup. The long oval fish platter is in constant use, even though it's not always used for holding fish. It looks beautiful with a rainbow of cooked vegetables arranged in horizontal lines, or with slices of fillet of beef, or a ham and veal loaf. Footed cake stands add interest and variety to a buffet.

We stock up on crocks and ramekins in many sizes. They are good for storing and serving everything—butter, relishes, jams, dips, ketchup, mustards, mayonnaise, olives. And a scoop of ice cream fits perfectly into a ramekin, which can be placed on top of a pretty dessert plate. If we had to choose one kind of glass, it would be a large all-purpose stemmed wineglass, and we would buy two dozen instead of eight each of three different types. We think all kinds of drinks—from orange juice to scotch on the rocks—look and taste better in a stemmed glass. Pitchers make a beautiful sculptural display; they are also in constant use. If nothing else, they keep the milk and juice cartons off the table. Our basic flatware is a contemporary off-white plastic-handled five-piece set which mixes well with our antiques and flea market finds. We like the way the off-white handles look with our white dishes. It isn't necessary for whites to match; indeed, different shades of white are pleasing together.

Baskets are convenient, decorative, versatile tableware; they are also beautiful stacked or left empty. For versatility, use straw cheese trays as place mats; consider nests of Chinese wicker trays as a set or individually. Marketing baskets, berry baskets, bread baskets, and Chinese steamer baskets hold fruit, vegetables, breads, jam jars, votive candles, flowers…the list is endless.

Under our plates we like to use paper lace doilies reminiscent of a French patisserie, small rag rugs, dish towels, or unfolded napkins. And a bare table can be very effective with just a place plate underlining the dinner plate.

Glassware

Plain or fancy, stemmed or otherwise, almost any glass can be pressed into service for any occasion. Consider iced tea in a wine-glass, wine in a French Picardie glass. The setting—and the dishes you use—often determine the perfect glass.

Stainless steel with rat tail porcelain handles

Stainless steel with rivets and black handles

French bistro silver plate

Stainless steel with ivory plastic handles

Flatware

This place setting (at right), currently being made in England by New York silversmith James Robinson, shows that the century-old custom of assigning twenty-five pieces of silver, each to a different task, is still in use today. It goes without saying that the place setting was not meant to be put out in its entirety, or that the table would be laid with silver from end to end. Besides, one would never need all these implements in the course of one meal; oysters, snails, and fish would never be on the same menu any more than there would be bouillon, cream soup, and vegetable soup together. According to Emily Post, no more than three of any implement should be put on the table at one time. If a fourth fork is necessary, as for dessert, add it when dessert is served. Edward Munves, the owner of the store James Robinson in New York, reports that a recent Philadelphia bride was given a service for twelve of this twenty-five-piece place setting by her doting parents. For most of us, however, it suffices to be aware of

A complete place setting in the Queen Anne pattern by silversmith James Robinson

1 Seafood Fork   2 Snail Fork   3 Pastry Fork   4 Dessert Fork   5 Salad Fork   6 Fish Fork

7 Luncheon Fork   8 Dinner Fork   9 Fruit Knife   10 Steak Knife   11 Fish Knife   12 Butter Knife

13 Cheese Knife   14 Luncheon Knife   15 Dinner Knife   16 Tablespoon   17 Iced Tea Spoon

18 Dessert Spoon   19 Sauce Spoon   20 Cream Soup Spoon   21 Bouillon Spoon   22 Fruit Spoon

23 Teaspoon   24 Ice Cream Spoon   25 Demitasse Spoon

the delightful variety of sizes and shapes available in forks, knives, and spoons. It is nice to be able to recognize an object on a flea market table or at a formal dinner, and to know its original intention. There are no longer strict rules governing flatware; a snail fork goes well on a pickle dish, a tablespoon makes an excellent serving spoon.

Today, the five-piece place setting is standard, and fulfills most of our needs. Other odd pieces can be added a piece at a time. We are partial to the silver-blade butter and cheese knives with colored handles that were made in England in the early 1900s, and use them on the table or for hors d'oeuvres. We are always on the lookout for old European tablespoons which are bigger than our American soup spoons and perfect for pasta. A collection of old serving pieces might include a pie slicer, a macaroni server (a cross between a fish slicer and a comb), and a round, flat, pierced tomato or cucumber server.

Flatware, old or new, plated or sterling, ornately turned, plastic handled or sculpturally simple: These are jewels of any table.

Napkins

Napkins change the look of a table more than any other single element, and so we have dozens of napkins—hundreds actually,

if one counts all the bandanas, scarves, dish towels, and washcloths that we also draft for service as napkins. It is far easier to

store ten sets of napkins than ten sets of dishes if you are partial to varying table settings. You can fold napkins, drape them, tuck

them into glasses, pull them through bracelets, or tie them with ribbon or raffia. The only thing we don't advise is draping them over the backs of the chairs; we tried that once but realized midway through the meal that we had been a bit too creative for our own good. No one had noticed the napkins and all the laps were napkin-less.

Table Settings

A table setting is easy enough to vary, and here we've used as our foundation a basic white buffet plate. Set on a paper doily with French bistro silver and a lace-edged napkin, the look is lovely yet simple; changed slightly with a Portuguese hand-painted fruit plate, damask linens, and Baroque gold-rimmed glasses makes a fancy affair of a meal. A more homey look is in the blue-

and-white pattern china on the rag mat, accented by the blue flatware and white fish silver. A country meal for company means adding a bold terra-cotta place plate and a matching terra-cotta bowl. The pretty napkin dresses up the solid feeling of the plates and wood-handled flatware.

MORNING SETTINGS

*B*reakfast can be as cheerful and lively as cornflakes with the kids, as sensually indulgent as breakfast in bed, as extravagantly stylish as a champagne brunch. During the week, the morning meal is a great setting for a business discussion, a committee meeting, a gossip with an old friend before the telephone rings and the day starts in earnest. But on weekends and on vacations, the morning meal becomes an occasion.

Morning settings are endlessly adaptable, not only to one's psyche but also to the season and the weather. A cold and snowy morning calls for a substantial meal served in a warm and cozy setting; a sunny summer day suggests light fruit eaten out-of-doors.

Breakfast foods are inherently beautiful, and one needs only to look to the food itself for decorative inspiration. Voluptuous muffins, crusty breads, a vivid rainbow of jellies, glass pitchers glistening with juice—such foods preclude the need for additional embellishment. Things of a kind make strikingly handsome compositions, whether it's a bowl heaped with eggs, a footed compote stacked with lemons, or a basket of oranges.

Especially important for the morning, when time is of the essence, is keeping staples stored in containers that can go from refrigerator or cupboard right to the table. Jars of jam are kept in a basket in the refrigerator, butter in a porcelain crock, sugar in anything that strikes your fancy. We decant and remove from cartons our potables as soon as they come from the store.

Most of us approach breakfast with minimal expectations. Therefore, when it is beautifully, thoughtfully, artfully presented, it is a very special treat, indeed.*

Hereafter, an asterisk appearing at the end of a description connotes a recipe provided in the recipe chapter.

BREAKFAST IN BED...*the ultimate luxury! When we spent a weekend at our friend's house in Westchester, New York, we didn't want to get out of the gorgeous faux bamboo bed. So there we stayed, with a large wicker tray-like basket lined and set with French jacquard napkins. Pierre Deux fabric-covered baskets lined with pretty paper doilies served up fresh brioches and sweet rolls. A larger version of the Pierre Deux basket set on the night table held coffee and sugar and cream.*

BREAKFAST IN NANTUCKET *at Carolyn and Roger Horchow's pine kitchen table seems to embody the very essence of an early morning in New England. Nantucket peasant bread, Morning Glory muffins, cranberry bog honey in a simple glass jar, local produce, and masses of flowers from the garden are set off by French faience hand-painted plates and heavy English flatware. The Horchow's collection of one-of-a-kind pewter mugs are used for coffee, and handmade New England goblets are used as eggcups. An eclectic combination of delicate porcelain bowls and all kinds of baskets is displayed on the sideboard. The maid and butler are American folk art cutouts originally designed to hold mail; here their trays hold cream and sugar.**

BASIC BOILED EGG BREAKFAST *transforms the most common ingredients into a still life in white. The whitest eggs, cradled in excelsior, are the focus of both the setting and the menu. The white ramekin contains butter, and white butter chips hold sea salt and cracked pepper. Old-fashioned double-sided egg holders, cotton napkins, and paper doilies are likewise white. The porcelain spoons (actually French tasting spoons) and milk-filled barrel tumblers (glasses commonly found in hotel bathrooms) complete the pristine setting. A basket or a bowl of eggs is a favorite centerpiece of ours; they're nearly always on hand and can be left out all day with no ill effects.*

BREAKFAST OF CHAMPIONS *can be as much fun as an elaborate Sunday brunch, but doesn't demand nearly as much effort. Wicker cheese trays from Spain serve as place mats, their handles knotted with oversize napkins. Milk is on the table in a simple laboratory glass jug. French jelly glasses hold freshly made juice; the juice oranges are heaped in a basket to bring a little sunshine to the table. In cool weather we buy our oranges by the case and set them out in baskets until squeezed or eaten.*

AUNT JEMIMA PANCAKE BREAKFAST *took place in the showroom of designer Willi Smith, an Aunt Jemima aficionado. This table setting tells you exactly what breakfast food to expect! Willi's collection of Aunt Jemima "kitsch"—cookie jars, salt and pepper shakers, syrup dispensers, and old oilcloth sign used as a place mat—stand out in vivid red-and-yellow glory against the backdrop of the all-white cityscape showroom.*

BREAKFAST IN A LUNCHEONETTE *is a fresh, appealing setting underlined with a distinct touch of nostalgia. This redone northern California restaurant looks like an updated 1940s eatery with its white enameled table, greenbanded to match the traditional green-banded restaurant dinnerware. The shiny old-fashioned toaster set directly on the table, the standard-issue sugar dispenser and salt and pepper shaker, and the classic Coca-Cola glasses all contribute to a look that is direct, honest, simple, and delightfully unpretentious. Popover pancakes, served right from the oven in individual cast iron frying pans, make unusual vessels for sliced fresh fruit.**

FRENCH BREAKFAST *is served up by our friend, Deanna Littell, a New York designer who lived in France for many years. The ficelles, long French breads here tied up with a blue-and-white gingham checked napkin, are the main course and the main decoration. The heavy blue-and-white tableware is reminiscent of that used in French homes and restaurants, as are the checked jacquard napkins, used as place mats and laid on the table diagonally to form a geometric pattern. Picardie glasses, commonly used for aperitifs in French cafés, are set out for juice. Other typically Gallic touches are the large café au lait bowls, the cocoa pot with wooden stirrer, and the pots of coffee served alongside pitchers of hot milk. Brown lump sugar in a chinoiserie teacup and butter in a mustard crock are wonderfully incongruous. The basket collection is arranged on the back wall like a group of paintings, and from time to time baskets are taken down and used for serving.*

BREAD AND BUTTER BUFFET *is an easy, appetizing way to have an early morning meeting. There's nothing to fuss with here so you'll be free to attend to the business at hand. All this breakfast takes is a pot of coffee, cream and sugar, and a variety of breads—from Italian to sweet—served up on anything from a wooden dough bowl or old breadboard to a classic egg basket. Strawberry and herb butter are in small crocks; glass bowls hold jams and preserves. A stack of small enameled tin trays with wooden butter spreaders serve as plates. Pretty flowers are casually arranged in a jug, and eyelet-edged napkins tucked into large coffee mugs are a fresh and personal embellishment.**

BREAKFAST BASICS *can be stored so that they are appealing enough to be presentable at the table, and don't have to be transferred to serving containers. You can keep a basket loaded with jam in the refrigerator; that way all you need to do is simply remove the lids and add the spreaders for serving.*

ALTHOUGH WE USE BUTTER *at almost every meal, it makes its first appearance of the day at breakfast, where we would never have the time to do it up right unless it were stored prettily to begin with. Besides, it really is more of a focal point*

at breakfast than at other meals. We keep our butter in a crock or ramekin that will hold one stick of butter, mounded. Then, after it has been whittled away at a meal, we transfer it into a smaller crock or butter chip, smooth it with a knife or fluff it with our fingertips, and put it away until the next meal. Hard butter looks great in rough slices on a flat plate. Softened butter can be made into balls with an ice cream or melon scoop, and pressed into a coeur à la crème mold, a terra-cotta pot, or a small canning jar. If you prefer using a stick of butter, choose an attractive, unique dish. Molded butter and butter curls are time-consuming and tedious and, I think, a bit too fancy for a pretty, homey effect. Choose a method for storing and serving butter that will look as good in the morning as when it was put away the night before.

SUNDAY BREAKFAST AT HOME *is often moved to our living room if we want to linger awhile, read the paper, or just lounge around on a comfortable couch. The Chinese wicker trays make breakfast an eminently moveable feast. Each tray is set with a croissant on a French hand-painted pottery dish, fruit in an oversized champagne glass and old hand-painted napkins. On the coffee table the ceramic croissant and brioche almost look like the real thing. We transported them from the refrigerator where they store a chunk of butter and a serving of jam.*

A HEARTY HUNT BREAKFAST *utilizes an amazing diversity of elements which harmonize to create the quintessential English country feast. The massive pine table is set with hand-painted French Quimper china, a chinoisserie bowl with jam, Indian cotton napkins, English stag-handled flatware, and hand-blown goblets from Vermont. A blue-and-white porcelain platter stacked with muffins and miniature banana breads is lined with heart-shaped galax leaves from the local florist. The handsome eighteenth-century English pine sideboard holds a lavish buffet. The look of abundance is epitomized by the cornucopia overflowing with melon slices, grapes, and plums, all wreathed in ivy from the garden. (Actually, this is a bowl-shaped basket tilted and weighted in place by a whole melon.) By picking up the colors of the eighteenth-century portrait, the food becomes part of a romantic still life.*

LATE SUNDAY BRUNCH *in the Connecticut countryside is a work of art by contemporary artists Judith and Robert Natkin. A gloriously bright pastel rainbow of majolica is the background; the plates on the table are a matched set from this extensive collection. (Majolica is the sturdy, colorful, English and American pottery that was produced for everyday use during the Victorian period.) The muted old rag place mats and the soft-hued Indian batik napkins are certainly different, but the varied patterns work well together because of the harmony in the color scheme. The cups and saucers, the footed dish with bread, and the cheese plate are all majolica. The meal is simplicity itself: papaya and wedges of watermelon, nut bread, cheeses, and hard cider in champagne flutes.*

BREAKFAST FOR TWO *centers around a pair of coffeepots that were originally intended as a tea service. The odd oblong plates are restaurant pickle platters, each big enough to hold a ramekin of butter, a slice or two of bread, and a wooden knife. The giant coffee mugs are really "kitchen mugs" designed for use by restaurant chefs to beat small amounts of sauces and dressings. The glass milk bottle, glass honey jar, and Mason jar with sugar came directly from the kitchen to the table, showing once again how neatly beauty and practicality go hand in hand.*

BREAKFAST IN THE BOARDROOM *has a business-like, no-nonsense atmosphere, conducive to serious debate and discussion. The handmade plates with a pattern that recalls men's suiting fabric and the crisp white man-size napkins have a serious, sober effect in this instance. The table arrangement is eminently practical; each place setting is self-contained with its own butter, jam, cream, and sugar so that the meeting can proceed without any interruption. In the center of the table, a square ceramic platter holds croissants; a large footed bowl looking like gray flannel is heaped with brioches.* →

BED AND BREAKFAST *is the order of the day at Casa Alma in the Pacific Palisades, a charming guesthouse that's part of the California bed-and-breakfast network. The table setting is uniquely and totally southern Californian, from the lush, semitropical foliage in the courtyard, to the bold, bright Mexican-inspired china, and these vibrant, multicolored folk art statues of Adam and Eve and the Tree of Life. Aebleskivers, wonderfully spiced raised pancakes served with powdered sugar and blueberry syrup, are the specialty of the house and the centerpiece of the table.* *

BREAKFAST IN AN ARBOR *is at the Sonoma Mission Inn in northern California's wine country. Lush local pink roses echo the color and pattern of the heavy French jacquard tablecloth and napkins. Straw cheese trays, here used as individual service plates, hold ramekins of butter, pots of jam, and homemade croissants. Oversized wineglasses half-filled with orange juice will be topped off by champagne waiting in the terra-cotta cooler to make the classic drink, mimosa. Pretty white doilies dress up the trays; a whimsical ceramic chicken holds sugar cubes.* *

SUNDAY BRUNCH *with Woodstock ceramicist Mamie Siegel bears witness to an artist applying her talents to her table.*
Much of the tableware, including the table itself, was handcrafted by the hostess. The table is a composition of handmade,
irregular ceramic tiles, and the plates are meant to be an intrinsic part of the table's design. Each plate has its own pattern which

corresponds to a matching pattern painted into the design of the table. It's this design that acts as a "place mat" for the companion plate. When the plate is removed its pattern remains. Table and plates are shiny, modern, Deco-like. The antique silver spoons are a pretty pastiche on this sleek surface.

When breakfast moves outside, the artist takes the same napkins that were rolled on the indoor table and overlaps them to create a tablecloth. She sets this with odd, fan-shaped handmade plates and mismatched mugs. The subtle harmonies and contrasts are done with an artist's eye: blueberries sit in the melon on the red plate and strawberries in the melon on the blue one.

NOON SETTINGS

*H*ow nice it would be if our noontimes were Europeanized so that two-hour lunches would be the norm. The happy custom of sitting down to a pretty table and a real meal at lunchtime, unfortunately, doesn't seem to fit our life-style.

Five days out of seven, we are at lunch in the middle of a frantic workday, whether at home or in an office. Therefore, the noon meal assumes a very special importance on weekends and holidays when there's nothing but anticipation beforehand and lingering satisfaction afterward. Whether it is a long, lazy summer lunch or a warm and cozy winter day, making the food and the setting appropriate to the season and occasion heightens the feeling of enjoyment and well-being.

On those other five days, with some forethought and a little imagination, a desk or a conference table can serve as a backdrop for a beautiful noon setting. If you work at home, or if home is nearby, a light lunch, interestingly arranged, is a welcome break in the daily routine. Efficiency and expediency are the watchwords here, but that doesn't have to mean a paper place mat, a tin-foil container and a styrofoam cup.

Lunch is the traditional time to do business; it may be a sophisticated hour for a tryst or tête-à-tête, or a charmingly continental way to entertain a group of friends. Each day's own particular set of circumstances dictates whether our noon setting should be matter-of-fact, romantic, elegantly formal, or just plain fun.

LATE SUMMER LUNCH *is the essence of simplicity and grace. A perfectly plain white ironstone bowl and oversized plates are strikingly appropriate to the untrimmed, uncut vegetables here. The fringed napkins add a softening touch, and the French plastic-handled flatware a bit of sparkle.*

COOL SUMMER LUNCH *is light, airy, and delicate: the very essence of a summery setting. The open pattern of the wicker table is seen through the glass plates; lace-like embroidered napkins give the same open feeling. When the food and the tableware are this pretty, there is no need for additional decoration. The melon in the center is heaped with sour cream dressing for the beautifully sliced fruit.*

AN AUTUMN LUNCH *is prepared by Giorgio DeLuca, famed food purveyor of Dean and DeLuca. In a bare loft setting a sumptuous, abundant clutter of food and serving pieces are inviting on the simple refectory table. Half a dozen vinegars and oils are always set out on the table. Fresh radishes make a striking still life—they practically glow on this pile of terra-cotta saucers. A remarkable arrangement of plump figs, pears, and grapes in a footed bowl are worthy of a Dutch master. A marble round underlines a thick stoneware mortar and pestle used to grind basil for the pistou, a peasant soup served here in shallow bowls. A wooden round holds bread and a crock of butter. Napkins are striped dish towels. The potted palm in a clay planter is another "centerpiece" that is placed well away from the center of the table.* **

A BUSINESS LUNCH AT HOME *is often served on the coffee table in our living room. Pots of geraniums sit in a basket tray; a set of oval Chinese straw trays are in lieu of place mats. The dark green bandana used as a napkin picks up the green band on the classic restaurant china. Chunky tea tiles catch drippings from a white wine sangria-filled pitcher and the old-fashioned seltzer bottle. Lemon chicken, cold string beans sesame, and pasta salad are arranged simply on each plate which is filled in the kitchen beforehand and placed on the trays so that guests are able to carry their own self-contained meal and setting. Best of all, no serving is necessary, and the well-arranged table makes a note pad and pencil convenient for a real working lunch.*

LUNCH AT THE DESK *takes place in spa developer Ed Safdie's vintage Manhattan high-rise office. Takeout orders of sushi assume remarkable grace when served on huge wood lacquered plates set directly on his glass-topped desk, accompanied by linen napkins and crystal wineglasses. Both chopsticks and silverware are set out. This easy elegance requires only clearing the desk of its papers beforehand.*

LUNCH IN AN ARTIST'S STUDIO *is great fun when the artist is Charles Bell, a photorealist who glorifies antique toys in his art. The same toys he collects and paints are used on his table; food and setting are equally light hearted. On the butcher block top, flowers pop out of 1940s tin sand pails and little windup toys of the same vintage stand guard. Old-fashioned gumball machines and blow-up creatures decorate the sideboard. Chairs, paper napkins, and plastic flatware are in bright crayon colors. White tin trays act as underliners for white restaurant plates. The three-foot-long hero sandwich is both the lunch and the centerpiece. Beer is iced in a galvanized tub, later to be poured into chunky glass mugs.*

A COLLECTOR'S LUNCH *is awash in color as sunlight filters through the vivid pastels of the glasses in the window. The rosy glow in the room is no accident, with just a little planning: pink accents can be traced in the pink flowers on the majolica plates, the rims on the contemporary service plates, the flatware, and the damask napkins. The burnished tint of the painted red early American table generates its own glow. Giant Spanish water glasses are hand-blown; the flaws and irregularities add interest and charm.* →

SCANDINAVIAN LUNCH, *served by Marimekko's children's wear designer, Kristiina Ratia, is casual, sunny, and direct. Bold simplicity, a hallmark of her profession, is evident in her table setting. Striped fabric is fitted to the table much like a contour sheet with elastic at each corner. Simple flat white restaurant ware plates with slightly raised edges hold the striped napkins, which are precisely arranged to follow the line of the tablecloth stripes. The heavy Italian stoneware footed plate presents a fresh fruit still life; by contrast the more delicate cake stand with the glass dome shows off cheese. The rolls are on chunky restaurant tea tiles, which were originally made to protect tables from hot teapots. Tall, heavy, hand-blown flutes can be used for wine, iced tea, beer, or water.*

LUNCH IN A NEW YORK STUDIO LOFT *takes place where textile and home furnishings designer Katja lives and works. Often she and a guest will eat at the butcher block kitchen work island in the heart of the studio. The setting is unassuming and uncomplicated. White rectangular French platters are placed directly on the wood surface. The makings for Scandinavian open-face sandwiches are on the large cutting board. Brightly striped washcloths of Katja's own design are folded in thirds and used as napkins. Beer goes into vintage ice cream soda glasses.*

CONFERENCE ROOM LUNCH *takes place at the Knoll International design headquarters in New York's Soho. In keeping with this company's high-style philosophy, the table setting is the essence of contemporary simplicity and pure design. At the end of the table, a large round of black glass holds a stainless steel bowl filled with peaches; more fruit and cheeses are placed directly on the glass. Flat terra-cotta pots of day lilies complete the "centerpiece," which is placed well away from the center of the table so as not to interrupt conversation and communication. The bread and butter plates are plain enameled tin trays; other table appointments are equally unassuming and straightforward.*

LUNCH FOR ONE, *a stylish indulgence of Dean and DeLuca's Joel Dean, is surprisingly sleek and sophisticated for a country house. Objets d'art form a sculptural grouping: Two glass Art Deco vases-cum-candleholders play against a brass vase with sea grass and a few blooms. The texture of the wood tray offers an interesting contrast to the striking sheen on the silver fruit plate. While soup is in an oversized white mug, savory basil pie sits happily on a colorful majolica plate. A rolled up dish towel serves as an oversized napkin.**

A FRENCH COUNTRY LUNCH *is in perfect harmony with its surroundings, even though it takes place in Lillian Williams's sunny living room in Sausalito, California. As the proprietor of the chimerical antique store La Ville du Soleil the hostess has immersed herself, both professionally and personally, in the eighteenth century. The table setting is evocative of a richly textured meal of a bygone era. Blue and white, in assorted combinations, make a lively, exuberant overall pattern. Gigantic footed soup bowls sit on white rectangular platters, a generous eighteenth-century soupière de Nevers is the tureen. Dried flowers in the vase are the same as those tucked into each of the curtain tiebacks. Straw place mats add a simple note; the two cavalier King Charles spaniels in the wing chairs wait for diners (and the sheep) to share the chairs with them.*

LUNCH IN SAN FRANCISCO *is served by Chuck Williams, originator of the fabulous cookware catalogue, Williams-Sonoma. A remarkable collection of personal treasures has been gathered by the host while on buying trips that take him around the world, and some are used here to complement the table setting and give it a polished and personal air. A dark blue Italian tureen with matching soup bowls holds potato and leek soup. Blue-and-white place mats are a lively contrast to the red-and-white check jacquard napkins. Breadsticks and wine are in bird's nest baskets. Antique English coin silver tablespoons, which are of a different pattern from the rest of the flatware, balance the country look of the setting. A very beautiful, very old, brass and porcelain samovar stands on a pedestal on the wall.*

INDOOR-OUTDOOR LUNCH *on eastern Long Island means the buffet table indoors and a table set for eating out on the deck. On the buffet, a long fish platter with a veal and ham loaf is lined with sprigs of rosemary. Three French Mason jars on a straw tray hold pickled cucumbers and onions, pickled tomatoes and onions, and pickled corn on the cob. Large tin kitchen spoons are servers. New potatoes vinaigrette are in an antique English creamery bowl, and a breadbasket neatly holds an assortment of mustards and wooden butter spreaders. The outdoor weathered wood picnic table is set with huge tin plates, oversized white cotton napkins, chunky Spanish glasses with just a hint of a green, and pots of sage. The pale green, gray, and white palette mirrors the hues of the dunes beyond and gives a cool look to a hot summer day.* *

CHEESE AND WINE, *the basic ingredients of a workday European lunch, are magically transformed into an occasion. We've chosen these cheeses not only for their taste and texture, but also for their marvelous shapes and colors. Arranging them was as logical as grouping the chunkiest and largest, creating a backdrop, eventually winding up with the tiniest goat cheeses in the foreground. Flower sprigs garnish the cheeses on the bed of galax leaves nestled in a large Chinese straw tray. The table is dressed up with paper lace doilies, lace-edged cotton napkins, and sprigs of wild flowers tucked into the wooden napkin rings.*

LUNCH ON THE DUNES *with Lee Bailey takes place at a table setting that harmonizes with the beach surroundings. Simple, everyday elements in natural materials and straightforward shapes work wonderfully with the weathered wood table. Covered terra-cotta clay pots hold salt, pepper, and grated cheese for the soup. A terra-cotta jug sprouts flowers. Perfectly plain tumblers are used for wine, white buffet plates for the food. The rich green escarole soup and the fresh green figs on a bed of dark, shiny leaves are fitting with the marsh grass in the background.* *

POOLSIDE LUNCH *on Shelter Island has a surprising opulence for an outdoor setting. Heavy oil-painted canvas fabric skirts the table to the floor, the deep-toned kilim pillows (brought outdoors from the living room) cushion the poolside chairs, and hand-embroidered napkins belonging to the hostess's grandmother grace the plates. Blues and roses from the pillows set the color mood for the table, along with the blue-patterned Italian crockery plates and jug. Pear possets in the basket open up to a first course of cold fruit soup; a stack of antique dessert spoons and a giant hibiscus create a romantic still life. A cluster of flowers picked fresh from the garden adorns each plate.*

LUNCH AT A COUNTRY INN *overlooking the sweeping vista of the Napa Valley, in the shade of a fringed raffia umbrella is heaven. The roughly hewn table only needed a simple setting, what with the natural beauty of the land. A clear glass vase holds a few wild flowers. One classic goblet is for water, adorned with a slice of fragrant lemon; the other holds a local Napa Valley wine. Pink cotton napkins seem to glow when set beside the white china dinnerware. The utter simplicity of this setting is no accident; it is merely a case of knowing when not to gild the lily!*

PICNIC IN A BAG *is a truly transportable one. One Sunday afternoon, in the Berkshire Hills on the way to the Tanglewood Music Festival, we picked up a glossy white shopping bag tied with a balloon. It was prepacked with everything we could possibly want for a lawn lunch. Each individual setting—plastic fork, knife, spoon, and paper napkin—was tied up with a ribbon. A charming bouquet of flowers had a great big bow. All five courses were arranged in clear plastic containers, from the freshly sliced mozzarella layered with sun-dried tomatoes and the smoked trout with sour cream sauce to the noodles with a Chinese sesame sauce and three kinds of cheese with fresh fruit. A tiny cup filled with mints was a delicious surprise. Everything was disposable, including the serving pieces. We only added wine, blankets, and the* New York Sunday Times.*

PICNIC IN A GARDEN *is a blatantly impractical affair. The backyard is as far as one would venture with this gorgeous, fragile composition, which is actually a table setting on a lawn. A black-and-white rag rug serves as a tablecloth, and black-and-white spatterware dishes hold the food. Tart plates hold asparagus tied with bows, pork chops, pâtés, and blueberry tarts. A wide-mouthed Mason jar, straight from the refrigerator, serves up the olives. Soup is in a classic white jug, and mustard is in a pretty crock. Day lilies, elegant and edible, decorate the salad. Old red-and-white country napkins with fringed edges and 1920s red plastic-handled flatware are bright notes. →*

RUSTIC LUNCH *that has a rugged, woodsy charm, beginning with the twig chairs and the weathered wood table, is appropriate in the country or any backyard. Rough plaid napkins, rustic hand-painted Italian pottery, painted wood napkin rings, and French flatware with handles that look like horn are all in harmony with the outdoors. Cinnamon sticks and orange slices flavor the iced tea in the heavy, faceted Italian glass tumblers; a chunky American glass pitcher holds more iced tea. The dessert, homemade raspberry tarts on a bed of leaves set in a cheese basket, the handle of which is wrapped with an ivy vine, serves as the centerpiece.*

LUNCH WITH A VIEW *at landscape designer Lisa Stamm's indoor-outdoor dining room on Shelter Island reflects the hostess's penchant for fanciful, unstudied arrangements. Here she uses her collection of bone bracelets as napkin rings; two thin voile napkins, one periwinkle and one mauve, are pulled through each ring and combined to create a third, lavender-like color. The round table is always kept covered to the floor with a chambray cloth of two-toned lavender. Hand-painted French pottery plates, each with a different crest, sit atop big blue glass service plates. The flatware is Sheffield. The flowers in the squat glass cylinder placed at the far edge of the table are a graceful extension of the garden just beyond.*

TEATIME SETTINGS

*T*eatime evokes so many wonderful images—a drawing room in an English manor house with a blazing fire, Alice in Wonderland with the Mad Hatter, Eloise reigning at the Plaza. And as for food, there is clotted cream, hot cross buns, currant-studded scones. There is the perfect English caper, conjured up in a cast of Agatha Christie characters ringing for the butler or the maid, at which time the murderer will be revealed.

Happily, teatime has found its way out of that rarefied literary atmosphere into the everyday real world, where it is fast becoming an alternative to the cocktail hour. Tea is a welcome respite and a great restorative, a delightful yet practical way to stave off hunger pangs if a late dinner is in the offing.

One of the nicest things about teatime is the opportunity to indulge yourself in a sinful, caloric concoction that you wouldn't dream of eating at an ordinary meal. Teatime is very much a treat time, and the setting should be fittingly fun and fanciful.

THE MAD HATTER'S TEA PARTY *includes the whole gang: Alice, the Mad Hatter, the March Hare, the Cheshire Cat, and the Dormouse. These whimsical cutouts, borrowed from the Jackson Tea Company of Piccadilly, inspired a witty tea table setting with a lace tablecloth, lace-edged napkins, and fluffy icing-topped cupcakes all in a row on little lace doilies. Huge white French café au lait coffee cups are for tea, ice cream soda spoons are stirrers, and sugar sits in a three-scoop*

sundae dish. Everyone has his or her own tiny Fiestaware teapot, each a different vivid color and shape. (Fiestaware is the bright American pottery of the 1930s, recognizable by the bands of concentric rings near the rim. Fiesta pieces always bear the Fiesta signature.)

AFTERNOON WORK BREAK *in designer Katja's studio is coffee or tea, Scandinavian style. The crisp, bright, geometric prints that are Katja's professional trademark are everywhere: in the bolts of fabric, on the couch and cushion, even in the tableware. A myriad of patterns form a unified picture because of the similarity of scale, color intensity, and mood. Mugs*

and cups are one-of-a-kind prototype designs, as are the napkins and the lacquered plate with cookies, here used with a second plate underneath to add height and importance. The cake is in a lacquered wood tray. Doilies add a delicate touch to the overall bold and graphic look.

THE ULTIMATE RESPITE *could be a quiet hour spent alone, having a sparkling, lemon-trimmed glass of mineral water, something crunchy and salty, a comfortable place to sit, and the latest magazines. Green leaf-shaped china plates and an abundance of fresh green leaves create a peaceful garden setting indoors.*

PIE AND COFFEE, *an Americanized version of English high tea, is especially inviting on a chilly afternoon. The dark green majolica plates have the same wintry look as the deep-toned Sgraffito pottery mugs from Italy, with their blue, mahogany, green, and brown raised pattern. The mugs are made by hand, and no two are alike; the jug holding the Queen Anne's lace and the cream-and-sugar set are of the same design. The taupe-and-white geometric jacquard napkins and the bone handles on the flatware have a creamy hue that blends with the Sgraffito. One-of-a-kind coffee spoons are silver. The old enameled spattered coffeepot has a pewter top with wood knob and handle. A bright strawberry-and-apple pie is in a Swedish wood box.*

HIGH TEA *in Abbie and Eli Zabar's Nantucket kitchen is a substantial affair, well suited to appetites near the sea. Herb tea in a glass teapot sits on a tea tile and filtered coffee is on the shelf below. Eli's famous shortbread cookies are center stage: heart cookies on a wood tray with heart cutouts, star cookies on a white dish. Goat cheeses are under a protective mesh tent. A French berry basket and white porcelain footed stand hold vegetables and fruit, and a handled wicker basket serves up bread. If the weather is inviting, a large wood tray can transport the entire tea to the deck outside, where it strikes an equally effective pose.**

NIGHT SETTINGS

Night ushers in a special kind of magic. Sunset, twilight, starlight, and moonlight shine outside; dimmed lights, spotlights, and most importantly, candlelight, make intricate patterns on nighttime tables, casting a sparkle that is unique to a nighttime setting. Our favorite night accessories are dozens of votive candles which we mass or scatter on our dining room table or sideboard. Casting their flattering light upward, the faces at the table look softer, prettier, and more romantic.

The glittery nighttime atmosphere enhances and heightens the sense of excitement and air of expectancy that surrounds the evening meal. Our workday is over; our mood and attitude shift, our alert daytime demeanor mellows.

Because the evening is imbued with a mood of anticipation, and often suffused with an enchanted glow, a table setting for these hours should be one to savor, to linger over, to relish. This is the time for candles, wine, and flowers; this is the place for your good crystal, silver— new or old—and service plates. Even the simplest or most country setting can convey the convivial qualities unique to a gathering of family and friends at dinner.

After all, dinner is the traditional time to be together and enjoy company. It is a time for relaxing, unwinding, reviewing the events of the day, and making plans for tomorrow. It is, more times than not, the highlight of the day.

Dinner is actually a reward for making it through the day—a daily, small celebration in a way. French statesman Talleyrand challenged: "Show me another pleasure like dinner which comes every day and lasts an hour."

But there really isn't one!

DESSERT ON A ROOFTOP *in Brooklyn Heights boasts a dazzling sunset in hues of blue, purple, and mauve with a table setting to match. The gleaming black lacquer table, the plum lacquer service plates, and the mauve lacquer dinner plates are the work of host Phillip Mueller, a craftsman who specializes in lacquering on wood. The napkins are berry-colored damask*

jacquard pulled through shiny silver napkin rings. Philip's grandmother's gold-rimmed wineglasses hold golden sauterne. Individual lilies, tucked into florist vials designed to hold a single stem, are interspersed among the fruit on the large lacquered platter.

WINTER DINNER PARTY *is warmed by brilliant, glowing pastels in pinks and roses. French Quimper dinner plates painted with a rosy rooster are set off by pink-rimmed crockery service plates and pink-handled flatware. Every napkin and every place mat is a different pattern but they work together with remarkable success, mainly because the colors blend well. Bright majolica saucers serve as wine coasters, and laboratory glass holds a procession of Queen Anne's lace. In the background, a cigar store Indian princess watches over all, and an abstract pastel canvas by Judith Dolnick seems to have been painted expressly to blend with the table setting.*

DINNER WITH CRAIG CLAIBORNE *takes place at his house in the woods of Long Island. The noted cookbook author is as sophisticated and correct about his table settings as he is about his food, and here he creates an aura of Victorian elegance and abundance. Each place setting has eight pieces of Christofle shell pattern silver, three wineglasses, and a Baccarat champagne flute. The blue-and-white-stripe men's shirting napkins are folded lengthwise and laid in the formal manner on the pewter charger. Paisley place mats are in Old World shades of plum, gray, and rose. Majestic pewter candlesticks and a silver wine bottle coaster add to the feeling of luxury and opulence.*

SOUP AND BREAD SUPPER, *all in snowy winter whites, shows off a fine collection of American and English antiques owned by Robert and Jane Cottingham. Although Robert Cottingham is a photorealist painter, Jane's passion as an antiques dealer sets the decor in their farmhouse. A Normandy bedspread is used as a tablecloth, its texture a charming counterpoint to the raised pattern on the rim of the old English ironstone soup bowls. The English silver plate knife and spoon is circa 1920. Small loaves of bread have been placed directly on old, heavy cotton napkins with an openwork edge design. Butter is in the small duck tureen, grated cheese in the small rooster, and the three large tureens in the middle of the table hold soup.*

← DINNER IN SOHO *takes place in Susan and Louis Meisel's loft directly above their New York art gallery; a loft as full of antiques and objets d'art as the gallery below. The pine table, so long it seems to go on forever, is set with a vivid collection of Fiestaware, and a random assortment of bright terry washcloths used as napkins. The salt and pepper sets are Fiesta, as is the bowl holding the small loaves of bread. Silverware is an incongruously ornate Baroque pattern, and the tumbler is standard restaurant ware. We ran fork tines over the butter to make a corn cob pattern, placed in the Fiesta pickle dish. The Meisels' invaluable collection of pottery, in simple shapes and bright colors, is striking here. The geometric-patterned jug by Clarice Cliff is English Art Deco, about 1930; the floral jug is Italian Lenci, also made about 1930.*

DINNER WITH AN ARCHITECT, *Charles Swerz, has a decidedly architectural quality. The striated Buccellati sterling flatware echoes the grooves in the decorative columns (one of which serves as a stand for the brushed and polished stainless steel wine bucket). Champagne flutes pick up the shape of the lilies in the glass vase. For contrast, a severe black marble table is paired with old desk chairs. Huge glass platters that serve as plates hold a first course of "drunken" shrimp. The whole look is softened by the antique lace-and-embroidered napkins, draped over the edge of the table.* *

COMPANY DINNER *in a carriage house on Long Island makes good use of a beautiful, extensive collection of small Hillstonia bisque baskets. On the table they hold bunches of marigolds and form a circle around the centerpiece, a glass cylinder filled with more marigolds. Other bisque baskets are displayed in the hutch. Simple large Wedgwood Drabware dinner plates are set right on the bare wood table, along with old damask monogrammed napkins, brass turtles, and tall brass candlesticks.* →

CRUDITÉ SUPPER *is pretty and delicious, winter or summer. In the hearty cold-weather setting, seasonal colors of red and green predominate, both in the tableware and the food. Green-banded oval luncheonette plates are layered on the bare wood table and red-and-white-patterned scarves are the napkins, tied with green-and-white cotton gingham ribbon. Asparagus, tied with the same ribbon, sits in a marketing basket along with an abundance of artichokes, kale, small tomatoes, and untrimmed carrots. A white porcelain tasting spoon is for serving the blue cheese dressing in the French porcelain bowl.*

In the summer, crisp white oval doilies, plain white oval plates, and Irish linen napkins with fagotted edges make for a light and airy look. Each setting has an individual custard cup with dip and a sprig of dill. The ceramic basket, which looks just like the real thing, holds a variety of vegetables—among them zucchini spears, baby carrots and baby asparagus, string beans, cherry tomatoes, radicchio, Japanese mushrooms, and a pot of chives for snipping. Hot green peppers are wrapped around the basket handle.

SUNDAY SUPPER *setting is early American country mixed with French country which is eminently appropriate at the home of* Country Living *magazine's art director and editor, Herb Bleiweiss and Rachel Newman. The table is a rich mosaic of patterns, from the famous Villeroy and Boch plates to the napkins in a variety of Pierre Deux fabrics. Place mats are typically American with their heavy woven fringe, and the tablecloth is sturdy curtain lace. An English fish fork and fish knife with bone handles are set for dessert at the top of the plate; these make a lively contrast with the plain English pistol-handled stainless steel. Majolica pineapple jugs, all in a row down the center of the table, hold sprays of Queen Anne's lace that echo the color, texture, and pattern of the ivory lace cloth.*

SAN FRANCISCO-STYLE SUPPER *is an altogether enchanted way to wind down the weekend. A white quilted mattress pad is put to use as a skirt for the table. Blue-and-white tattersall dish towels are set the long way as place mats; folded in thirds, they are also used as napkins. Our antique family fish forks and fish knives are used here, along with a giant tablespoon placed upside down in the European fashion. Chunky pillar candles and candleholders add height and dimension to the table.*

ANTIQUE-FILLED DINNER *has the signature Old World charm of Barbara and Mel Ohrbach, owners of the New York shop Cherchez. A hand-embroidered square tablecloth barely overlaps the top of the round table, and the napkins are embroidered antiques. The Ohrbachs put into practice what they preach: Old linens, lovingly used and properly cared for, will fare better than those stored away and unused.* →

SPARKLING, SHIMMERING, *richly textured settings always draw attention, especially when done by Silver Palate co-owner Sheila Lukins. Wedgwood plates, topped by Grandmother's Bavarian fish plates, go right on the shiny bare travertine table. Chunky green-stemmed Rhine wineglasses are paired with thin delicate balloon goblets. The flowered porcelain menu card is washable and has a bud vase stem. Other roses are in a variety of small vases, one of them being an uncapped saltshaker. The ornate flatware and the napkin rings holding damask napkins are both sterling silver, and the dessert spoon above the plate is for lime mousse. An antique openwork lace tablecloth covers the sideboard, and a lace napkin is a lining for the wood basket filled with peasant breads. Particularly appropriate to summer is the poached salmon on a long oval fish platter, and a glass bowl of basil-scented pasta salad.**

SUNDAY SUPPER BY THE FIRE *can be as simple and cozy as soup, bread, and some good wine. The overall setting is elegant and pretty, made up of pieces from different countries and time periods. Huge round Delft platters lined with French jacquard napkins are used as trays; the dinner plates hold French faience soup bowls. Antique Irish glasses etched with a grape leaf design, oversized pewter soup spoons, and wonderfully fat breadsticks are the only other accoutrements. The patterns of the table setting seem a scaled-down version of the welcoming chintz armchairs.*

← WINTER SUPPER *setting at artist Jeremiah Goodman's house in East Hampton, Long Island, is a composition of deep, masculine colors. Large brown crockery plates and brown plastic-handled silverware go with blue-and-white dish towels folded into squares and set on the plates. The same dish towel is tied casually around the wine carafe. Chunky green-tinted pilsner glasses complement the solid, handsome look. Silver baby porringers are used as ashtrays, and tall pewter candlesticks at the end of the table are arranged and balanced with the spiral wooden candlesticks and art on the fireplace mantel.*

WESTERN SUPPER *is bright and bold at Ralph Lauren's Colorado ranch. The table cover is ticking stripe, with washed-out denim mats that look like blue jeans. Big bright plaid napkins are folded once lengthwise so that they will hang casually over the edge of the table. Giant red ceramic charger plates (also called service plates) contrast with green goblets big enough for a bird to bathe in. Plates set on the charger plates are natural wood; they hold bowls filled with Charley's chili, capped with a baked cornbread topping. Sterling flatware is inspired by native American silvercraft, reminiscent of a silver conch belt. Wild flowers sprout from the milk bottle, and the crock holding the sour cream looks like a small ceramic pail. The salt and pepper shakers are natural wood with red enameled tops.* *

RED, WHITE, AND BLUE *is the appropriate color scheme here in this country feast set by Americana expert Mary Emmerling in her authoritative, authentic, American country style. Old blue American spongeware pitchers hold masses of daisies, the white bowls are filled with oranges and berries. Rough cotton homespun place mats are blue-and-white check; red-and-white homespun napkins are pulled through twig napkin rings. The flatware is a really beautiful hand-wrought pewter. Mary has strewn painted wood fruit in the center of the table and placed a line of heart-shaped candles in heart-shaped tin molds. Giant tumblers have playful wood swizzle sticks with heart tops.*

CHILI AND TORTILLAS, *set out on a sideboard, is an easy and delicious way to entertain; this kind of simple, hearty menu naturally inspires an American country setting. Chili is in a huge white ironstone chili pot, and a collection of yellow slipware bowls hold the trimmings for chili—chopped tomatoes, grated cheese, green peppers, and onions. Stacks of blue-and-white spatterware bowls reflect the collection of antique spatterware on the shelf below. We've filled old glass milk bottles with red and white wine. Checked napkins are rolled and tucked into glasses, and a napkin lines a painted American tray. Pewter tablespoons are the only utensils necessary. An antique spatterware jug is filled with daisies and a wrought iron drying rack for corn is an interesting bit of Americana. The wreath is fashioned from chili peppers.*

SEAFOOD SUPPER ON A DECK *is a simple affair: The setting takes shape from the goodness of the just-steamed lobsters and grilled corn. Shiny pewter plates, navy-and-white bandana napkins, lobster crackers shaped like lobster claws, and individual ceramic ramekins with melted butter are practical, and practically all you need. Groups of votive candles are in each corner, and a bandana-lined basket is filled with biscuits. In the center, an oval wicker tray is stacked with corn cooked in its husk over the grill. A white ceramic bowl holds lemon halves, and terry washcloths are rolled in a terra-cotta bowl and topped with lemon slices.*

CHINESE TAKEOUT *never looked quite so good. Two lengths of dish toweling-by-the-yard are used as runners crisscrossed at the center of the table and hanging over the edge. Bamboo trays are the place mats, complete with a matching dish towel rolled and tied with raffia, votive candle, Chinese export carp bowl, a cup for tea and small teapot, chopstick rest, and individual ramekin of hot mustard sauce. Chinese food containers—straight from the restaurant—fit snugly in two willow boxes; we asked for an extra container and filled it with flowers. Blue-and-white Chinese vases stand in the corner of the table.*

MOROCCAN EXTRAVAGANZA *is an exotic statement involving rich intricate patterns in muted colors. Rather than use a kilim as a floor covering, we've draped it over the coffee table platform. Blue-and-white batik napkins, each in a different print, tie up the silverware. Terra cotta is used as a base here—in the dinner plates, the crock for the couscous broth, baking dishes for the chicken and vegetables, and the tiny string-tied bowls used for salt and pepper. Gray stoneware bowls are for food and condiments; a huge stoneware bowl holds the couscous. We've used a Chinese tray (one of a nesting set) for a stoneware pitcher of wine and wineglasses; a smaller tray in the set is filled with votive candles. Other trays are filled with baklava and placed on a cake stand, and on the sideboard holding terra-cotta demitasse cups and coffeepot. The wooden spoon with holes is actually an olive spoon from Portugal used here to serve chicken. Two terra-cotta saucers, one inside the other, have a decorative arrangement of sliced oranges and an orange peel rose.*

CHARCUTERIE SUPPER *is a spontaneous, simple sausage-and-mustard spread. From our collection of pigs we've taken our giant wood pig box, lined the inside with packing straw, and placed five kinds of mustards in their own jars. A white plastic kitchen board holds breads and sausages which can be cut right on the surface with simple utilitarian kitchen knives. Cornichons are in white bowls, and individual carafes, usually used as bedside water containers, hold wine. Wood breadboards shaped like oversized slices of bread are used as plates. Since this meal isn't served at the dining table, dish towels used as napkins are practical as well as pretty because they cover your entire lap. And because the food is all finger food no utensils are necessary. If you don't happen to have a giant pig, mustards can be equally attractive in a simple baguette basket, lined with straw or a cloth napkin.**

TROMPE L'OEIL *is the background and the theme of this setting. A unique hand-painted screen by Richard Neas imitates a crowded kitchen cupboard, and the table has been set with witty references to the screen's colors and composition. Dishes are blue-and-white porcelain, very much like the "plate" in the painted cupboard; a blue-and-white print underskirt is covered with a simple white tablecloth. Dark green pressed glass goblets and dark green restaurant napkins standing in a brass napkin ring echo the "cupboard" colors. The placement of the candlestick and the tall green carafe with flowers seems to draw the entire table into the composition of the still life screen.*

THE FIRST ASPARAGUS OF THE SEASON *is always a reason to celebrate, and here it's taken to an extreme. A large trough-shaped asparagus platter is the centerpiece, and bunches of raw asparagus, tied with pink-and-red luncheon napkins, serve as decoration. Antique asparagus plates are at every place—even the wine decanter is modeled after asparagus. There's no reason you can't make something edible a decoration and have the serving ware the highlight of your table.**

DINNER FOR TWO *is as fresh and crisp as the Granny Smith apples lined up on the long fish platter, and as clear and sparkling as Perrier water with lime. Green-and-white dish towels are used as place mats and napkins, the latter rolled into wooden bracelets. Plumber candles go into the apples which are cored just deep enough to hold the candles steady.*

PASTA PRIMAVERA *is a lovely evocation of spring, and the table setting, as well as the food, is a deliciously fresh combination of white and springtime green. Muslin napkins with heavy white cotton lace go well with the unbleached damask tablecloth. Layered place settings include a paper doily, a twig trivet, a dinner plate, and large pasta bowl. The twig napkin rings and stag-handled flatware make an interesting contrast with the large Art Nouveau silver-plated spoon. Tulips, whose colors echo those in the pasta, are in a white ironstone pitcher. A French muffineer, usually used for powdered sugar, is used here for grated cheese. Tiny gold-topped salt and pepper shakers are like those found on first class airline service.*

SUMMER SUPPER *on the New York City terrace of graphic artist Richard Giglio is a careful composition contrasting mainly Chinese utensils with Italian food. Odd as the combination may seem, the match really does work. The mood is Oriental, seen in the rice-steamer baskets used for the place settings, porcelain spoons for holding sauce, and chopsticks. For accent, there is flatware in a bamboo pattern and goblets for wine. The ice cream soda glasses are used for water. Making the best of a small space, the Chinese wicker tray is set on the terra-cotta flower pot with a simple, delicious meal of risotto, hard-boiled eggs, and a hunk of Parmesan cheese. Lemons and limes add a bit of bright color. Pots of fresh herbs, tomatoes, and an abundant basil plant (complete with a scissor and knife for snipping and cutting) are lined on the terrace ledge. A white rectangular platter holds a salad of string beans and mushrooms. Richard has used yet another tray—this one is twig—for some prosciutto and melon.* * →

FRUIT IN THE ARMOIRE *includes whole poached apples, poached Seckel pears, and oranges in red wine, all in tall glass cylinders. Anjou pears are in a glass soufflé dish. Pressed glass footed dessert dishes and ornate silver spoons complete this still life, as glowing as a Van Eyck painting.**

BEACH PICNIC AT SUNSET *was a breeze when we transported everything in a wicker marketing basket on wheels, including the pink paper parasols. An Ohio Amish patchwork quilt, circa 1910-1920, sets the color scheme. A Chinese export tin wine cooler is painted with a cabbage rose which pairs nicely with the tiny bouquets on the enameled mugs. The color is also picked up by the pink-and-white plaid cotton napkins. The crockery pail keeps the soup warm until it goes into the mugs.*

Omelet in a "bread box" (frittata-filled bread), which is kept hot by multiple layers of foil wrapping, is served on a round breadboard. Wood, both in the bowl for the white and purple radishes and the square block for the cheese, is easy and durable. White tin plates, hardy restaurant wineglasses, and a big kitchen saltshaker complete the alfresco scene. *

FRESH FRUIT DESSERT *is presented in two different ways. A do-your-own-berries buffet sets out blueberries in an old blue colander, raspberries in a white tin colander, pitted cherries and strawberries in stoneware bowls. The cake stand, lined with a doily, holds individual shortcakes for serving with the berries; a footed bowl holds mounds of fresh whipped cream. Blue-and-white plaid napkins are folded into triangles and fanned out in front of a stack of stoneware bowls with blue tin spatterware spoons.*

In the more formal setting the same fruits are layered in tall wineglasses with thin slices of lemon and lime twisted on top, and served with large European tablespoons. Tea tiles are used as saucers, and pillar candles are on white china stands. The antique sugar shaker in the foreground is cranberry glass as is the tiny round box holding crystallized ginger. A stack of cranberry-colored paper napkins stands next to the old white ironstone sugar bowl. Decanters, one faceted and the other plain, hold after-dinner liqueurs.

MOST GOOD RESTAURANTS *follow a rather simple, but intentionally unobtrusive style for table settings. Their policy aims at the minimal in design: plain white china, a basic pattern in either stainless or silver-plated flatware, and good but unpretentious glassware. Quite rightly, this type of setting blends easily with most any kind of meal, including colorful sauces and garnishes.*

TABLE SETTING AT AUBERGE DU SOLEIL *in Napa Valley, California, is the prototype of elegant restaurant presentation. These are the kinds of classic restaurant appointments that are equally and timelessly correct at home as well: a crisp white tablecloth and simple large white plates, good, heavy silver-plated flatware, solid unpretentious glasses, and flattering pink napkins folded in the prescribed formal manner. There is nothing costly or unusual here, but the abundance of flatware (seven pieces in a place setting), wineglasses, sparkling decanter, and pretty flowers all evoke the anticipation of a special meal.*

TABLE SETTING AT ROBERT'S RESTAURANT *in San Francisco uses the same basic element as the Auberge du Soleil, but has an informal air. The classic white tablecloth here has a rose underskirt. Simple large white dinner plates are attractive with their fluted borders, especially when paired with the standard restaurant ware glasses and flatware which is quite sturdy. The overall look is spare and crisp, from the single rose and standard five-piece place setting to the napkins tucked casually into single wineglasses.*

TABLE SETTING AT THE SOHO CHARCUTERIE *in New York City is a reinvention of the classic white-on-white theme of more traditional restaurants. The patterned white tablecloth and napkins are the same as those found in French restaurants. The single white plate is actually a giant buffet plate. The fresh corn salad has been arranged back in its*

husk, with the leaves pulled apart slightly, giving it an airy, open look. A simple glass storage jar, Queen Anne's lace in a glass vase, and off-white-handled flatware are some of the elements contributing to the fresh, country look. *

TABLE SETTING AT THE QUILTED GIRAFFE, *New York City, is unique and luxurious, and a lovely departure from the basic white restaurant school design. Proprietors Susan and Barry Wine are renowned not only for their superb food but also for their unique presentations. A wide range of high-styled tableware is used in varied and unusual combinations, creating a rich and personalized look. The settings are decidedly correct in the continental mode with the European silverware placed face down and only a place fork and place knife set on the table; silverware appropriate to each course is brought when the dish is served. The napkin is folded into three crisp pleats and properly placed on each plate.*

Oriental influences abound; like the food itself, the settings draw on two worlds for inspiration. Gold-patterned Chinese dishes might be used for appetizers at one meal, as butter plates at another. Service plates are a rich deep maroon, sometimes used alone, other times as the bottom layer of an eclectic combination. Cinnabar, peach, and black are the colors on the table no matter the style or pattern of the individual pieces.

The goblets with unusual twisted stems are another deviation from regulation restaurant ware. The salt-and-pepper is anything but a matched set: The pepper mill is a utilitarian, precisely made stainless steel grinder, while the saltshaker looks like a tiny Chinese ginger jar in gold. This effective pairing of East and West, formal and informal, ornate and simple is typical of the world of the Quilted Giraffe.

133

HOLIDAYS

*H*olidays are a time for tradition and each holiday has its own personality, its own style, its own raison d'être. Most holidays come complete with a whole set of well-established customs and rituals, and often the food and the decorations—even the hour for the meal—are precisely prescribed.

The Fourth of July is always red, white, and blue. Thanksgiving means turkeys and pumpkins, dried wheat and leaves. Christmas wouldn't be Christmas without wreaths and mistletoe, shiny red apples and spicy aromatic punch, bowls of cinnamon and nutmeg, and all-over colors of red and green. New Year's Eve celebrations are (naturally) at the stroke of midnight.

If one starts a holiday setting with the basic holiday ingredients and then adds personal touches and family treasures, the occasion assumes an even richer significance. Holidays are a time to perpetuate the continuity of the family as well as the continuity of national, ethnic, and religious customs. The sight of Aunt Lavinia's punch bowl holding the perennial New Year's Day eggnog imparts a sense of permanence, familiarity, belonging.

A holiday meal is an at-home affirmation of enduring traditions, and the table setting is the natural structure upon which the occasion is celebrated.

EASTER TEA *is a pastel fantasy at our friend's house in Sag Harbor. Pink plates, peach napkins, lavender rag place mats, and blue teacups are the same pretty pale shades as the traditionally colored Easter eggs in the frilly compote dish. The silver candy dish has sugared almonds of the same hue, and a lavender and periwinkle pastel platter holds candied pineapple. The whimsical Art Deco teapot is part of a collection of personal miscellany brightening the table; china roses and a china fish are scattered about, and a pastel trivet cushions a painted pitcher filled with milk. A footed butter dish makes a big deal out of a pound of butter, and a blue Fiestaware bowl holds the wine bottle. On each plate, a leaf cradles a hard-boiled egg. A giant painted carved wood pig presides over this charming rite of spring.*

← VALENTINE'S DAY DESSERT *is all hearts-and-flowers at tableware designer Diane Fischer's house. The black lacquered table is set with red velvet free-form heart place mats; black ceramic vases are filled with lilies, roses, and freesias, all in white. Silver-coated almonds are in individual tiny red baskets, and a silver bowl holds red foil-wrapped surprises and heart-shaped cookies. For fun, two napkins are pulled through each silver napkin ring, a black one on the outside, a printed one inside. Black square glass service plates were a flea market find. Service plates are silver, as is the large European dessert fork. White china cups have a silver holder and silver saucer.*

FOURTH OF JULY CELEBRATION *is an unabashedly patriotic red, white, and blue supper. Americana stars-and-stripes bed quilts cover the two picnic tables. Blue-and-white dish towels are tied in a knot around red plastic knives and forks; the clothespins are for clipping the "napkins" to clothes in case of a strong wind. Religious, or seven day, candles are tall cylinders with poured tallow and are the most practical outdoor illumination as their flames are shielded from the wind. The light willow basket holds two plastic liners filled with wild flowers. A chunky glass cylinder is stacked with sliced tomatoes and*

onions. *A simple berry box, lined with a dish towel, holds mustard jars surrounded by baby's breath. The Vermont-made berry basket holds long breads, and an American spongeware bowl is filled to the brim with potatoes vinaigrette. Steak slices are arranged on a long fish platter and corn grilled on the cob, already buttered, is served in an antique American basket. The piéce de resistance is the flag-waving dessert: A white sheet cake, baked, transported, and served in an ordinary roasting pan, is spread with whipped cream and decorated with halved strawberries and whole blueberries.* *

THANKSGIVING DINNER *is a glorious celebration of the earth's rich bounties. For place mats, we've used giant leaves that we found growing outdoors. Scooped-out underripe pumpkins with the longest, prettiest stems we could find are used as soup bowls; a giant green pumpkin acts as a tureen. The sterling silver soup ladle, ornate silver coaster under the decanter, linen napkins with open fretwork, silver flatware, and paired crystal goblets are elegantly incongruous with the more earthy*

elements. We've decorated the sideboard with nuts, berries, and ivy vines trailing off the edges. Fruit, pie, and little pecan tarts are presented on footed dishes. The main course is a traditional turkey, and a long fish platter is filled with vegetables. The round peasant bread is monogrammed easily by cutting initials out of stiff paper, pinning them to the top of the bread, sprinkling flour over all, and then removing the paper.

THE TWELVE DAYS OF CHRISTMAS *are symbolized by these twelve brown paper bags filled with a variety of dried fruits and nuts; a charming tradition borrowed from Provence and set down on our coffee table in New York City. Each bag is rolled down, tied with either a red or green ribbon, and kept refilled throughout the holiday season. A bunch of grapes sits alongside the paper bags on the large flat basket.*

SCANDINAVIAN CHRISTMAS EVE *is gay and informal. A red tartan wool square covers the table, and red-and-white check gingham napkins are tied with a tartan ribbon. Continuing an at-home mood, each white dinner plate is ringed with an unadorned bleached twig wreath. Fat pillar candles of varying heights sit on a large round platter covered with galax leaves. The appetizer is as irreverent as the setting—baked potatoes, sour cream, and caviar with a sprig of fresh dill.*

CHRISTMAS CHEER *in the form of a festive snack is a cheerful welcome for drop-in guests. Bright red apples are piled in a stoneware bowl, with a pillar candle rising from the center. Green bandana napkins, sparkling glasses, a crystal decanter of sherry, and a chunk of Cheddar cheese on a breadboard are the very picture of holiday hospitality.*

REMINISCENT OF A RUSSIAN CHRISTMAS, *candlelight gleams in the majestic brass candlesticks, tall samovar, and extra-high cake stand topped with a doily and strawberry tart, extravagantly ribboned in red moiré. A brass basket is lined with a doily and filled with chocolate-dipped strawberries. The porcelain toast rack holds small embroidered napkins. French bistro cups and saucers are forest green with gold edging. A pressed glass restaurant sugar bowl holds brown crystallized sugar, and a cranberry glass-etched box holds crystallized orange rind. Peach-rimmed dessert plates are paired with silver fish forks. A deep red antique paisley scarf provides a spectacular sweep of color and intensifies the table's glow. →*

FOR AN INTIMATE NEW YEAR'S DINNER *we have created the aura of a Flemish still life painting. Combining the glitter of gold doilies and ribbons with the soft glow of candles set among Bosc pears, green apples, and bundles of fresh asparagus, a scene of subtle abundance is created at our pine table.*

NEW YEAR'S EVE DINNER IN BED *is the most indulgent celebration of all! This silver tray takes on additional sparkle from three layers of glass dishes and pearl-handled silverware. Wineglasses are filled with ice surrounding vodka shot glasses; dishes hold tiny buckwheat crêpes. The cut crystal creamer is filled with melted butter and the sugar bowl holds sour cream. Two small faceted glass bowls hold red and black caviar. An Italian damask towel is spread under the tray. It goes without saying that the bed linens are as beautiful, elegant, and fine as the occasion.* →

CELEBRATIONS

Celebrations are happy occasions, meant to commemorate milestones with festivity. Unlike settings for other meals, those intended for celebrations should have a custommade look, tailored precisely to the particular occasion and to the person or people being fêted. At its very best, a celebration should have a one-of-a-kind setting, a unique and personalized tribute to the "why" and the "who" of the party.

The recognition of a turning point or a landmark in one's life deserves special treatment. That treatment might be masses of flickering candles, glittering confetti, bouquets of flowers, clouds of high-flying balloons. It is the extra, out-of-the-ordinary ingredient that transforms a casual gathering into a memorable event.

Time, effort, imagination, and forethought are all important elements in making a successful celebration. Even an impromptu party can be a gala as long as you are willing to take that extra step toward making an extra special setting.

IMPROMPTU BIRTHDAY PARTY *was occasioned by our friend Ann's phone call that she had just arrived from Italy—and our realization that it was her birthday. We rushed to the bakery and bought the fanciest cake we could find; we gathered up all the flowers in the house and put them together in two blue-and-white Chinese vases. On our old standby, the porcelain menu card, we wrote the "Happy Birthday" message. Then we put everything on the table in the hall to surprise her as she came in the front door.*

← TABLE FOR ANY OCCASION *is the all-chocolate dessert buffet, the ultimate in sweets. A museum quality heirloom tablecloth sets the stage. Brownies, dressed up like cupcakes here, were baked in muffin tins lined with glassine bakery doilies. A two-layer chocolate cake filled with whipped cream has a spectacular looking design on top, easily achieved by sprinkling powdered sugar through a doily. A double chocolate cake is surrounded by lumps of rock candy, and a brass cake stand shows off nutty brownie bars. A muffineer filled with powdered sugar is for further sweetening, as are the brown sugar cubes in the pressed glass old-fashioned ice cream sundae dish. Carved ivory-handled dessert forks, English ironstone wheat pattern coffee mugs, the new ironstone coffeepot, and the old ironstone teapot create a bland vanilla foil to the rich brown edibles. Bavarian gold-rimmed dessert plates are hand-painted, each with a different design. Hydrangeas create an Old World hedge. **

FIRST BIRTHDAY PARTY *is an adult fantasy of any baby's ideal celebration. Two white wicker high chairs stand ready for the birthday baby and special guest; other chairs will be filled in according to age and size of the revelers. A piece of heavy white vinyl is thrown over the table with the "Happy Birthday" message written in red and blue magic marker. A group of skinny candles, tied with a ribbon, are stuck into the cake to make one flame. Terry washcloths are an inspired idea for napkins, bright red ceramic plates are colorful, and white plastic mugs, eminently practical. Chinese food takeout containers, one for each little guest, are filled with red jelly beans. A cloud of white helium-filled balloons hovers overhead—a sensational decoration and surefire distraction for when the novelty of the food and the table starts to pall.*

SWEET SIXTEEN PARTY *was a mock formal, sit-down dinner as a gift to our friend Tracy on the occasion of her sixteenth birthday. Tracy made the guest list and chose the menu; we did the rest. We were the staff and we dressed for our roles: Peri was the waiter, Charley played chef, a son Benjie was the butler. Each place setting had a votive candle illuminating a small porcelain menu card with the date and the guest's name written in gold. Small glass decanters were scattered down the center of the table with the appropriate, traditional pink roses and purple freesia. Crocheted cotton place mats and lacy napkins added to the fresh, young, feminine feeling.*

COUNTRY WEDDING PARTY *celebrated our friends Peter and Hester's marriage outdoors on a sunny summer day. The picnic table was slip-covered in flowered chintz, and the plain three-tiered white cake was decorated with real flowers to match those in the chintz. The cake is on a large white platter fitted snugly into a heavy basket tray. The marketing basket was filled with paper plates, paper hand towels for use as napkins, and plastic forks. A white bain-marie, usually found warming sauces in restaurants, acted as the wine cooler. A basket under the table was filled with silver and gold disposable champagne glasses; the rest of the champagne, in an ice-filled tub, was next to it.*

SILVER ANNIVERSARY PARTY *couldn't be anything else but! A stack of white saucers with silver foil heart doilies are for the dim sum that sits in a traditional Chinese steaming basket. A collection of sentimental silver baby cups hold the sauces. The champagne flutes are tied with silver bows, and the candle glow comes from these ice cream-shaped candles.*

BON VOYAGE DESSERT *has a nostalgic, romantic air, reminiscent of a luxurious cruise ship. Wedgwood shell pattern plates, circa 1850, are set on classic white plates. The nautilus shell in the center of the table, filled with grapes and vines, is of the same vintage. Strawberries and madeleines are in shell bowls, and a smaller shell is filled with sour cream. Tiny individual shells are filled with brown sugar for dipping strawberries. A beautiful antique lace tablecloth pulls together this pretty farewell party.* *

TRIPLE-TIERED DESSERT PARTY *is a festive concoction which owes much of its charm to a mock three-tiered table. We actually used one table and two cake stands stacked one on top of the other, each one holding a white platter securely in place with florist's clay. The bottom table is massed with bunches of grapes and strawberries and ice cream sundaes with long skinny candles. The second tier has an assortment of individual fruit tarts. The top tier holds a magnificent whole pear tart.* →

CELEBRATIONS ARE FUN AND EASY, *especially when you remember that a single touch like fresh flowers or playfully long candles (or little short ones) can turn the simple into the sublime.*

RECIPES

It seems as if everyone was a gourmet cook in the 1970s. Nothing was too much work or took too long to prepare. Simply put, we had become a sophisticated food society. But when friends arrived for dinner, often we were too exhausted to enjoy their company. Fortunately for food and friendship this trend in cooking has changed direction, and we are no longer working hard to create elaborate meals. Today we enjoy foods that are light and simply prepared. Most importantly, we are cooking with seasonal and regional goods which have their own naturally good taste.

On the following pages are some of our favorite recipes and those of our friends. They all have three ingredients in common: They aren't complicated, they don't take a great deal of time to prepare, and they are tasty. Here, then, is to good food and good company.

Candied Bacon

A real breakfast treat for anyone who wakes up with a sweet tooth.

1/4 pound dark brown sugar
1 pound bacon, at room temperature

Heat oven to 350°. Spread the brown sugar on wax paper. Press each strip of bacon into sugar, coating both sides. Arrange flat on 11-by-13-inch jelly roll pan. Cook for about 30 minutes. Remove from oven. Using 2 forks (it will be scalding hot—do not touch) roll each strip of bacon, jelly roll style. Place on a china plate to cool before eating.

DEPENDING ON YOUR GROUP, ENOUGH FOR 4-6 PEOPLE

Breakfast Hash Browns

These hash browns are tangy when made with leftover Potatoes Vinaigrette.

3 tablespoons butter
1 onion, sliced
Potatoes Vinaigrette (page 177)

In large skillet, melt butter. When hot, add onions and potatoes. Sauté until golden brown.
Serve with eggs (any style) and sausage, ham, or bacon.

Morning Glory Muffins

The combination of fruit and nuts makes these hearty and sweet muffins from the Morning Glory Café on Nantucket a wonderful breakfast treat.

2 1/2 cups sugar
4 cups flour
4 teaspoons cinnamon
4 teaspoons baking soda
1 teaspoon salt
1 cup raisins, plumped in brandy and drained
1 cup coconut, shredded
4 cups shredded carrots
2 apples, shredded
1 cup pecans
6 eggs
2 cups vegetable oil
1 teaspoon vanilla extract

Sift dry ingredients into a large bowl. Lightly dust the raisins with flour. Add the coconut, fruit, and nuts, and stir well. Add the eggs, oil, and vanilla, stirring only until combined.
Spoon batter into cupcake tins and bake at 375° for 20 minutes. Muffins should "ripen" for 24 hours for maximum blending of flavors.

MAKES 16-20 MUFFINS

Popover Pancake

This pancake is spectacular to serve, delicious to eat, and easy to prepare. It is equally enjoyable when served in pie slices for dessert, as it is when presented whole for a hearty brunch.

¹/₂ cup flour
¹/₂ cup milk
2 eggs, lightly beaten
4 grinds or 2 shakes of nutmeg
4 tablespoons butter
2 tablespoons confectioners' sugar
Juice of ¹/₂ lemon
Fresh fruit or jam (optional)

Heat oven to 425°. In a mixing bowl combine the first 4 ingredients and beat well with rotary beater.

Melt butter in a cast iron enamel-coated 8-inch omelette pan with heatproof handle (this is the only pan in which the pancake sides rise and puff up). When the butter is very hot (sizzling) pour in batter. Cook on top of the stove over medium-low heat for a few minutes to set. Do not stir. Bake in oven for 20 minutes until puffy and golden. Sprinkle with sugar and return to oven for a few more minutes. Sprinkle with lemon juice and serve at once, with fresh fruit or jam, if desired.

SERVES 1 VERY HUNGRY PERSON FOR BRUNCH
SERVES 4 AS DESSERT

Aebleskiver, Danish Raised Pancakes

An aebleskiver pan is a cast iron "frying pan" with indentations the size and shape of a small orange. It is a must for this recipe.

4 cups flour
1 tablespoon sugar
1 teaspoon salt
1 teaspoon ground cardamom
3 tablespoons double-acting baking powder
3 cups milk
4 eggs, separated
1/3 cup beer
Juice of 1/2 lemon
Grated rind of 1 lemon
Shortening
Confectioners' sugar

Combine the first 5 ingredients in a large bowl. Mix together the milk and egg yolks; beat into the dry ingredients. Add the beer, lemon juice, and rind. Beat the egg whites until stiff, but not dry, and fold into the batter.
Heat the aebleskiver pan and put 1 teaspoon of shortening into each well. Test heat by dropping in a little batter; if it forms a shape immediately the shortening is ready. However, the pan should not be so hot that the pancakes brown too quickly and remain uncooked in the middle. Put only about 1 rounded tablespoon of batter in each well. When batter becomes golden, turn with a fork and cook on the other side, about 5 to 6 minutes. Drain on a paper towel. Refill well each time with more shortening. Sprinkle with confectioners' sugar.

MAKES ABOUT 4 DOZEN PANCAKES

FRUIT BUTTERS

Fruit-flavored butters are tasty with warm breakfast muffins and breads, and surprisingly good on biscuits served with lunch.

Strawberry Butter

1 stick (8 tablespoons) sweet butter
4 ripe strawberries, cored and sliced
2 teaspoons dark brown sugar
Pinch of salt

Place all ingredients in bowl of food processor and blend for 1 minute. Spoon into a small ramekin, mounding the top.

Orange Butter

1 stick (8 tablespoons) sweet butter
2 teaspoons grated orange rind
2 teaspoons orange juice
1 teaspoon dark brown sugar
Pinch of salt

Follow directions given above for Strawberry Butter.

Buckwheat Crêpes with Caviar

Not all pancakes are homespun breakfast fare. These savory crêpes, served with crème fraîche and dotted with black or red caviar, represent sheer pancake elegance for all occasions.

1 egg, at room temperature
1 1/2 cups milk, at room temperature
3 tablespoons sweet butter, melted, warm
1/2 teaspoon sugar
1/2 teaspoon salt
1/2 cup buckwheat flour
1/2 cup all-purpose flour, sifted
Vegetable oil
1 cup crème fraîche
1 jar (2 ounces) black or red caviar
Lemon wedges (optional)

Whisk egg until light and foamy. Then gradually whisk in the milk, the melted butter, the sugar, and salt. When thoroughly combined, gradually add buckwheat flour and all-purpose flour to egg mixture, stirring with a whisk just until flours are moistened; do not overmix. Let batter stand, covered, at room temperature for at least 1 hour. Brush a 6-inch crêpe pan or small heavy skillet with a thin film of vegetable oil; heat over medium flame until a few drops of water sizzle several seconds when splashed on pan.

Pour 2 tablespoons of batter into pan; immediately tip pan and rotate to cover bottom evenly with batter. Pour any excess back into bowl. Cook until edges begin to brown and batter is set, about 1 minute.

Turn crêpe, using a flexible spatula; cook until underside is speckled with brown spots, about 30 seconds. Remove crêpe to ovenproof plate; cover loosely with a towel and keep warm in the oven set at lowest heat. Lightly reoil pan, if necessary; continue to make crêpes until all batter is used, stacking them as they are made on plate in oven.

Serve with the crème fraîche and caviar on the side, and with lemon wedges if desired.

MAKES 16 CRÊPES

Chuck Williams's Leek and Potato Soup

Cool and delicious for a warm summer's day.

4 to 5 medium leeks
1 medium onion
2 tablespoons unsalted butter
4 medium potatoes
4 cups chicken broth, preferably homemade
1 cup milk
1 cup heavy cream
Minced fresh parsley and chopped tomato (or pimiento)
 for garnish

Trim, wash, and slice leeks (discard tops); peel and slice the onion. Melt butter in a large saucepan, add leeks and onions, and sauté slowly for 10 minutes or until transparent, stirring occasionally. Peel and dice the potatoes, add to leeks together with the broth. Bring to a simmer and cook for another 15 minutes or until potatoes are tender. Scald the milk and add to the vegetables. Bring to a boil, season with salt and pepper, then put through a food mill or purée in a food processor or blender. Chill thoroughly. Before serving swirl in the cream. Garnish with minced parsley and bits of chopped tomato or pimiento.

SERVES 6

166

Lee Bailey's Escarole Soup

The secret of this simple soup is in the chicken stock. The flavor of the final dish can be no better than the stock you start with. If you use canned stock, enhance its taste by simmering it down a bit (15 minutes or so) with a large onion chopped in it and maybe a stalk of celery. Strain these out before using.

1 medium head escarole, washed
6 cups rich chicken stock, preferably homemade

Salt and pepper to taste
Parmesan cheese

Tear carefully washed escarole leaves into bits, discarding the tough bottom parts. Add this to the stock and simmer for about 15 minutes or until escarole is tender. Correct seasoning with salt and pepper if necessary. Serve with Parmesan cheese on the side.

SERVES 6

MARINATED VEGGIES

The heart of the summer and into early fall, when vegetables are plentiful and inexpensive, is the ideal time to prepare marinated or pickled vegetables in large quantities; better still, they are welcome at the table any time of year.

Marinated Cucumbers and Onions

2 cups warm water
1 cup white wine vinegar
¹/₄ cup sugar
1 teaspoon salt
5 large cucumbers
2 medium onions

Combine water, vinegar, sugar, and salt in a glass measuring cup.

Peel cucumbers only if the skin is tough. Slice into ¹/₄-inch rounds. Peel and thinly slice onions.

In a glass storage jar, alternate layers of sliced cucumbers and onions. Add brine, and marinate for at least 1 hour before serving.

To store, refrigerate, then allow to return almost to room temperature before serving.

MAKES 2 QUARTS

Pickled Beets

A tangy addition to any green salad, especially one prepared with fresh arugula. We also like to keep these on hand to add to a French-style crudités course. Serve small portions of julienned carrots, shredded celery root, potatoes vinaigrette, sliced cucumber, and the pickled beets. Add a quartered hard-boiled egg to each plate. This is a satisfying salad for lunch, or a hearty first course for dinner.

30 medium beets, peeled
1 teaspoon salt
5 tablespoons tarragon vinegar
3 teaspoons sugar

Place the beets in a large saucepan, and add just enough water to cover.

Add salt, 3 tablespoons of the tarragon vinegar, and sugar. Bring to a boil and continue cooking for 30 minutes, or until the beets are fork-tender. Do not overcook. Cool for 30 minutes in the liquid.

Remove beets, reserving cooking liquid. Slice or dice beets into bite-sized pieces. Spoon the beets into a 2-qt. storage jar.

Into a measuring cup pour 1½ cups of the remaining liquid and remaining 2 tablespoons tarragon vinegar, and combine. Pour mixture over the beets in the jar. Marinate at room temperature for at least 1 hour, turning the jar several times. The beets will keep refrigerated indefinitely.

MAKES 2 QUARTS

Marinated Tomatoes and Onions

Use a 2-quart (or 2-litre) glass storage jar. The type shown in the photograph is good for both serving and storing. Neatly layer tomatoes and onions, then spoon on "dressing." This makes a delicious lunch, or a "salad" course for dinner. Serve with warm French bread.

8 medium tomatoes, ripe but firm
4 medium onions
1 cup chopped fresh basil (if fresh is not available, omit)
1 teaspoon salt
Freshly ground pepper to taste
2 teaspoons sugar
¼ cup green olive oil
½ cup balsamic vinegar

Slice tomatoes into ¼-inch to ½-inch-thick-slices. Peel and slice the onions into ¼-inch-thick rings. Layer tomatoes and onion rings in a jar, sprinkling each layer with basil. In a measuring cup, combine salt, pepper, sugar, olive oil, and vinegar. Mix with a fork and pour over the tomatoes and onions. Marinate at room temperature for at least 1 hour before serving, turning jar several times. Will keep refrigerated for three days; after that the tomatoes get too soggy.

MAKES 2 QUARTS

Giorgio DeLuca's Soupe au Pistou

This Provençal (Niçoise) vegetable soup is perfumed with a heady pistou of basil and garlic. Bon Appétit!

2 carrots, peeled and chopped
3 leeks, sliced (tender white parts only)
5 medium potatoes, diced
1 pound fresh white beans (or 1 can white navy beans)
Bouquet garni of thyme, parsley, and celery leaves
1 cup elbow macaroni
1/2 pound green beans, cut into 1 inch lengths
3 zucchini, coarsley chopped
1 tablespoon salt

PISTOU

4 to 5 cloves garlic
1 cup fresh basil leaves, roughly chopped
1 cup extra-virgin olive oil (preferably Antinori)
1 fresh tomato, diced
Salt and pepper
1 cup freshly grated imported Parmesan cheese

Cook all of the vegetables, except the green beans and zucchini, and the bouquet garni in 3 quarts water in a covered casserole over medium heat for 30 to 40 minutes. Add the macaroni, green beans, zucchini, and salt, and cook uncovered 15 minutes longer.

Prepare the pistou. Combine the garlic, chopped basil, and cheese in a mortar and pestle. Grind slowly. While grinding slowly drizzle in the olive oil, then add the tomato, salt and pepper. Grind until mixture has formed a rough paste.

When soup is ready stir in 3 to 4 tablespoons of pistou to the pot.

Serve in large soup bowls, with the pistou on the side to be added according to taste. Parmesan may also be sprinkled on top, according to taste.

SERVES 6

Charley's Chili

Topped with a cornbread crust, here is a new way to spruce up an old favorite which we make in simple ovenproof restaurant ware bowls. It's an especially sturdy dish for a hungry group.

6 cups of your favorite chili recipe, heated
1 cup yellow cornmeal
1 cup all-purpose flour
¹/₄ cup sugar
4 teaspoons baking powder
¹/₂ teaspoon salt
1 cup milk
1 egg
¹/₄ cup melted butter
Sour cream for garnish

Heat oven to 425°. Put 1 cup of heated chili in each bowl, or to come 1 inch from top of your bowl.

Combine the cornmeal, flour, sugar, baking powder, and salt in a mixing bowl. Add the milk, egg, and butter. Beat with a fork until smooth, about 1 minute.

Place bowls filled with chili on a cookie sheet. Pour batter over hot chili just to cover. Bake for about 25 minutes, or until crust is golden brown. Serve steaming hot, with a dollop of sour cream atop each bowl, and a bowl of sour cream on the side.

SERVES 6

Charley's Chunky Tomato Sauce

A fast and spicy sauce to top pasta, polenta, or seafood.

3 tablespoons extra-virgin olive oil
4 cloves garlic, minced
1 onion, finely chopped
1 can anchovies, drained and coarsely chopped
8 sun-dried tomatoes, coarsely chopped
Pepper to taste (no salt)
1 35-ounce can peeled whole Italian tomatoes, drained
  and chopped
1/2 cup chopped parsley
1 tablespoon herbes de Provence (thyme, rosemary, oregano)

Heat oil in a large skillet, and in it briefly sauté the garlic. Add the onions and sauté for 2 minutes. Add the anchovies and sun-dried tomatoes; continue to sauté for another 2 minutes. Add freshly ground pepper (about 8 turns), the tomatoes, parsley, and the herbs. Simmer for 5 minutes.

MAKES ENOUGH SAUCE FOR 4-6 SERVINGS

Gil's Barbecue Sauce

A sweet and spicy sauce for ribs or chicken. Serve with a Caesar salad, or red and yellow peppers with purple onion in vinaigrette, plus fresh corn and herb butter.

1/2 pound (2 sticks) butter
1 clove garlic, pressed
1 small onion, chopped
1 teaspoon salt
Freshly ground pepper to taste
1 tablespoon sugar
1 1/2 tablespoons lemon juice
1/2 cup tomato ketchup
1 tablespoon Worcestershire sauce
1/2 teaspoon Tabasco sauce

Mix all ingredients together in a large saucepan. Cover, bring to a boil, reduce heat, and simmer for 5 minutes, stirring occasionally.

MAKES ENOUGH SAUCE FOR 4 CHICKEN OR DUCK HALVES, OR 2 RACKS OF RIBS

Mustard Vinaigrette

This is a very pungent full-flavored dressing. The flavor can be altered by using different oils and vinegars.

3 cloves garlic
1/2 teaspoon salt
1 teaspoon freshly ground pepper
3 tablespoons Dijon mustard
6 tablespoons balsamic vinegar
1/2 cup olive oil
1/2 cup vegetable oil

Mince garlic. With the back of a chopping knife, mash garlic and salt together and place in a 2-cup glass storage jar. Add the pepper, mustard, and vinegar, and blend. Whisk in the olive oil, then the vegetable oil until blended. Let vinaigrette mellow for at least 1 hour.

MAKES 1 1/4 CUPS

Dill Mustard

This is a sweet and pungent mustard. It goes well with charcuterie, cold poached shrimp, or gravlax.

1/2 cup rough whole-grain mustard
1/2 cup Dijon mustard
1 teaspoon dry mustard powder
3 tablespoons brown sugar
3/4-1 cup chopped fresh dill, loosely packed

Combine all ingredients and blend with a fork. Store in a glass jar with a tight lid. Will keep indefinitely in refrigerator.

MAKES 1 1/3 CUPS

Soho Charcuterie's Corn Salad in Husk

It is so pretty to serve this corn salad in its original container, the husk.

Kernels from 8 ears white or golden corn, 3^1/2-4 cups
4^1/2 cups inexpensive dry champagne or white wine
2 roasted red or green bell peppers, cut into strips 1 x ^{1}/8-inch
4 sun-dried tomatoes (Pumate San Remo), drained and minced
^{1}/2 cup olive oil from the sun-dried tomatoes
2 heaping tablespoons minced fresh chives
^{1}/2 teaspoon salt
Freshly ground pepper to taste

Remove ears from husk carefully, without destroying the husk. Remove silk from inside husk. Prepare salad: Bring 4 cups of the champagne to a simmer in a medium-size saucepan, add the corn, and cook at a simmer for 5 to 7 minutes, or until the kernels are just tender, still slightly undercooked. Drain, spread the corn out on a plate to cool, and sprinkle with the remaining champagne.

Transfer the corn to a serving bowl, add the remaining ingredients, and combine gently but thoroughly. Stir occasionally, if you are not serving the salad immediately. Place husks on individual plates and scoop salad inside, overflowing a little.

SERVES 8

Spinach Capellini

The surprise in this dish is the zesty flavor of fresh lemon slices.

4 tablespoons butter
3 tablespoons olive oil
6 cloves garlic, sliced about ^{1}/8-inch thick
3 pounds fresh spinach, washed, patted dry, stems removed
^{3}/4 teaspoon salt
Coarsely ground pepper to taste
1 thinly sliced lemon, seeded
Juice from ^{1}/2 lemon
^{1}/2 cup chicken broth
1 pound capellini #9 (use dried pasta)
Freshly grated Parmesan cheese

Use a large heavy skillet, and heat the butter and olive oil until bubbly. Add the garlic and sauté on medium-low heat until nut brown, but be careful not to burn. Add the spinach, salt, and pepper and toss, using large tongs. Sauté until spinach is slightly wilted, about 3 to 4 minutes. Add sliced lemon and toss, cooking another 3 to 4 minutes. Combine lemon juice and chicken broth and add to the spinach.

In 4 to 6 quarts of boiling salted water, cook the capellini until just tender, about 3 minutes from boiling point. Drain, and divide among individual bowls. Spoon spinach-and-lemon broth over capellini.

Serve with a bowl of freshly grated Parmesan cheese.

SERVES 4 AS A MAIN COURSE

Ted Weiant's Picnic Noodles with Sesame Sauce

A delightful surprise for a picnic—or any other time. Packed in clear plastic containers, these flavorful noodles are easily transported for dining alfresco.

6 to 8 large cloves garlic
1 cup unsalted chunk-style peanut butter
1/2 cup soy sauce
1/2 cup dry white wine or sake
4 teaspoons sesame oil
3 tablespoons hot chili oil
6 tablespoons or about 1/2 cup minced fresh cilantro, reserve some for garnish
6 to 8 tablespoons sugar
1-pound box spaghetti (or pasta of your choice)

In a food processor, blender, or bowl chop the garlic—you should have about 4 tablespoons. Add the peanut butter, soy sauce, wine, and 3 teaspoons of the sesame oil. Process until thoroughly blended. Add the chili oil, cilantro, and about 3 to 4 tablespoons of the sugar. Process and blend again. Adjust sugar to taste. Allow sauce to "ripen" for several hours or overnight. Sauce keeps indefinitely and improves with age.

Cook spaghetti until barely tender and still a bit firm. Drain in a colander and rinse under cold water; drain well. Spread out on a clean kitchen towel and pat dry. Put in a large bowl and toss gently with remaining 1 teaspoon sesame oil. Chill. Before serving, toss again with a little sesame oil, if desired, and cilantro.

For taking on a picnic, you could combine the sauce and noodles at home, or package them separately, and let each person help himself.

MAKES ENOUGH FOR ABOUT 6 PEOPLE

Omelette in a Bread Box

For a cool weather picnic, take along a hearty omelette, kept warm inside its own "bread box."

1 large round French bread (10 to 12 inches in diameter)
2 tablespoons olive oil
2 tablespoons butter
4 medium new potatoes, washed, dried, and thinly sliced
1 medium onion, diced
2 cloves garlic, mashed and chopped
2 medium zucchini, thinly sliced
9 eggs, beaten well
3/4 teaspoon salt
Freshly ground pepper
3 rounded tablespoons Parmesan cheese

Heat oven to 350°. Cut bread in half horizontally. Partially hollow out center of each half, leaving about 1 inch of soft bread and crust. Melt the oil and butter in a 10-inch omelette pan. Brush about 1 tablespoon of the oil and butter inside bread halves. Reassemble loaf and wrap in heavy foil. Place in oven while preparing omelette.

Add potatoes, onion, and garlic to the pan, turning often, about 4 to 5 minutes, over medium heat. Add zucchini and sauté for about 3 minutes. The potatoes should be nicely browned and the zucchini translucent.

Add salt and pepper to beaten eggs and pour over vegetables. Cook omelette over low heat, pushing edge of the omelette toward the center so that the runny eggs run off and begin to set. Cook until the top is just set, but still moist. Run a spatula around the edge, adding a little butter to loosen the omelette from the pan. Sprinkle grated Parmesan cheese over top of the omelette. Then, place the pan in the oven and heat for 6 minutes to set the eggs. Remove the bread from the oven, open and slide omelette into bottom half of bread, then quickly replace top to form a box. Wrap in several layers of heavy foil to keep toasty warm for hours.

SERVES 6

Felipe Rojas-Lombardi's Roast Pepper, Basil, and Cheese Pie

PASTRY CRUST—ONE 8-INCH SHELL

1 1/2 cups all-purpose flour
3/4 teaspoon salt
6 tablespoons sweet butter, chilled
2 tablespoons Crisco or vegetable shortening
1 to 2 tablespoons ice water

ROASTED PEPPERS

4 red peppers (1 1/2 pounds)
3 tablespoons olive oil or vegetable oil

CUSTARD

4 eggs
2 egg yolks
2 cups heavy cream
2 ounces goat cheese
2 ounces grated Gruyère, Emmenthaler, or Jarlsberg
1 teaspoon salt or to taste
8 tablespoons thinly sliced scallions (white part only)
1/4 cup tightly packed basil leaves, thinly shredded
1/2 teaspoon fresh hot chili pepper (seeded and finely chopped) or
   1/2 teaspoon dry chili pepper
8 to 12 perfectly uniform fresh basil leaves for garnish

Prepare the dough. Place the flour and salt in a bowl. Working quickly, slice the chilled butter thinly and add to the bowl along with the shortening. Using fingertips, swiftly incorporate flour with butter and shortening until mixture forms a mealy or crumbly texture. Sprinkle with ice water a little at a time and knead mixture into a smooth ball. Place in plastic wrap and refrigerate for a half hour. Remove dough from refrigerator and place on a lightly floured work surface. Using a rolling pin, flatten the ball of dough into a 1-inch-thick, 6-inch-round slab; proceed to roll it out to an even 1/8-inch-thick circle. Gently fold the circle in half and in half again to form a quarter circle. Place into an 8 1/2-inch pie tin and open the folded dough carefully and evenly, allowing a 2-inch measure of dough to hang down from the edge of the pie tin. Using your fingertips, lightly press the dough to the bottom and edges of the pie tin. Gently roll the hanging dough upwards toward the edge of the pie tin, and with a fork, press down to form a neat design around the pastry shell. Prick the bottom of the shell with a fork and line with a sheet of foil or parchment paper. Fill this liner with plenty of dried beans and bake in a preheated 400° oven for 15 minutes. Then turn heat down to 350° and bake an additional 15 minutes. Remove beans and liner and continue to bake for 15 to 20 minutes or until crust is lightly golden. Cool on a rack.

Rub the peppers thoroughly with the oil. Place on a rack and into a preheated 500° oven for approximately 1/2 hour, turning to roast peppers evenly. When peppers are done—they will collapse—remove from oven. When cool enough to handle, cut each pepper in half with a paring knife. Using a teaspoon, remove seeds and gently pull away the stem and skin with your fingers or a paring knife if necessary. Be careful to leave the flesh intact. Sprinkle very lightly with a pinch of salt and roll each half-pepper. You should end up with 8 rolls about 4 inches long. Set aside.

Finally, make the custard. In a bowl, beat the eggs and egg yolks, then add the heavy cream. Crumble in the goat cheese and add along with the grated Gruyère, salt, scallions, shredded basil, and hot pepper. Mix thoroughly. Gently pour mixture into prebaked pastry shell and garnish the surface with a spiral design of roasted red pepper rolls. Place into a preheated 350° oven for about 45 minutes or until set. Remove from oven when done, and immediately place the whole basil leaves between the red pepper rolls in an alternating pattern. Brush surface lightly with olive oil and allow to cool for 10 to 15 minutes before serving.

SERVES 6

Richard Giglio's Risotto

Serve this risotto with soft boiled eggs which have almost cooled, a platter of sliced garden tomatoes, and slices of thick country bread, toasted after having been spread with olive oil. Pass a bowl of freshly grated Romano cheese.

8 tablespoons butter
1 onion, chopped
2 cups Italian Aborio rice
5 cups homemade chicken broth, or canned
1 cup grated Parmesan or Romano cheese (use 1/2 for serving at the table)

Sauté chopped onion in 4 tablespoons of the butter in a heavy saucepan until transparent, but not brown.

Add the rice and continue to sauté until rice takes on a bit of color, about 4 minutes.

Heat broth to a boil in a separate saucepan; then keep at a simmer. Begin adding broth a little bit at a time (about 1/2 cup), and stir until the broth is absorbed.

When the rice is cooked, but still *al dente*, remove from heat. Stir in the remaining 4 tablespoons of butter, plus 1/2 cup of the cheese.

Transfer to a large heated platter. Serve hot.

SERVES 4

Asparagus with Lemon Butter

In season, asparagus lovers make a whole meal of asparagus, the plainer the better.

2 pounds young asparagus
1 teaspoon salt
2 sticks (16 tablespoons) lightly salted butter
3 teaspoons grated lemon peel

Juice of 1 lemon
8 thick slices of a good white bread

Use a skillet or fish poacher large enough to accommodate the length of the asparagus. Wash asparagus and break off stalks where they snap most easily. Put 2 inches of water in pan, add salt, and bring to a boil. Add asparagus to pan. Return water to a boil, cover, and cook for 2 minutes, or until asparagus are tender but firm. Remove from water and drain asparagus on a clean kitchen towel.

While you are waiting for the water to come to a boil and cooking the asparagus, melt the butter. Add lemon, juice and grated lemon, and blend. Toast the bread and place on four warmed plates. Arrange the asparagus on top of the toast and drizzle with lemon butter. Serve at once.

SERVES 4

Note: Vinaigrette is also good on hot or cold asparagus as an appetizer or salad course.

Steaming Broccoli Vinaigrette

A surprising taste for hot broccoli.

1 large head of broccoli
1 tablespoon salt
1/3 cup vinaigrette

Trim broccoli and cut into bite-size flowerettes. In a large steamer pot (preferably with a colander insert) bring the water to a boil and add the salt. Add the broccoli and return to a boil; let boil for 1 minute and remove broccoli. Quickly shake off excess liquid, then place in a warm bowl and toss with the vinaigrette. Serve hot.

SERVES 4

Twice-Cooked Potatoes Vinaigrette

A potato lover's dream, tangy potato salad the first day, incredible hash browns the next morning for breakfast.

5 pounds very small new potatoes
1 to 2 tablespoons salt
Mustard Vinaigrette (page 172)
Fresh dill, chopped

Wash potatoes and cut in half, but leave the skin on. In a large pot, bring salted water to a boil and add potatoes. Boil just until fork-tender, but not soft. Drain in colander (do not rinse); transfer potatoes to a bowl large enough to hold all 5 pounds. While potatoes are still hot, drizzle over them a generous amount of mustard vinaigrette. Add the rest of the potatoes, drizzle more vinaigrette over top layer, and sprinkle with dill. Cover and let marinate at room temperature until ready to serve, shaking bowl occasionally to coat all potatoes, adding additional vinaigrette if needed.

FOR A PARTY OF 12-15 PEOPLE

Veal and Ham Loaf

Served at room temperature and thinly sliced, this loaf is a light meat course, ideal for a warm weather meal.

2 pounds ground veal
1 pound ground ham
2 teaspoons salt
1/2 teaspoon freshly ground pepper
1/2 teaspoon dried thyme (if fresh thyme, use more)
2 eggs lightly beaten
2 tablespoons Cognac
1 1/2 cups seasoned bread crumbs
Fresh rosemary or other herbs for garnish

Heat oven to 350°. In large bowl, mix all ingredients together. Grease a large roasting pan. With your hands, shape a loaf as long as the pan, but only about 5 inches wide to create a long narrow loaf (like a fillet of beef). Bake 2 hours. Cool in pan. Loosen bottom with spatula, and remove carefully. Slice about 3/8-inch thick. Arrange sliced loaf on a fish platter (or other long platter). Garnish with fresh rosemary or other herbs or leaves.

SERVES 10

Pickled Weisswurst

We like to include this with a charcuterie assortment for a hearty cocktail party, or at an informal wine tasting. Serve with a good variety of mustards, a bowl of cornichons, and crusty breads.

1 1/2 cups water
1 cup white wine
3/4 cup tarragon vinegar
2 carrots, scraped and thinly sliced
1 teaspoon mustard seeds
1 teaspoon whole allspice
1/2 teaspoon whole peppercorns
6 bay leaves
3 cloves garlic, crushed
8 weisswurst

Combine all ingredients, except weisswurst, in an enamel saucepan, and simmer for 5 minutes. Slice weisswurst into 1/2-inch rounds, and remove casing. Add weisswurst to poaching liquid, then remove pan from heat. Cool in poaching liquid to room temperature.
Transfer to a glass cylinder vase or storage jar for storing and serving. Serve at room temperature.

SERVES 8-16

Curly Pasta Salad

We love pasta, in all shapes and in all seasons. Here is a
tasty warm weather salad.

1/2 box fusilli (1/2 pound), cooked until tender
2 hard-boiled eggs, chopped
3 stalks celery, diced
1/2 onion, chopped

4 sun-dried tomatoes, chopped
Mustard Vinaigrette (see page 172)
Salt and pepper

Combine fusilli, eggs, celery, onion, and tomatoes. Add
enough vinaigrette to moisten and flavor the salad. Salt
and pepper to taste. This is best when left to marinate for
an hour or so, covered, at room temperature.

SERVES 4

String Beans Sesame

These string beans have an Oriental flavor which we like to serve with Lemon Chicken, or on a salad plate combined with potatoes vinaigrette and sliced tomatoes.

1 pound young string beans, washed
4 teaspoons sesame seeds, toasted
1/3 cup soy sauce
1/3 cup dry white wine
1/4 cup water
1 teaspoon balsamic vinegar
1 clove garlic, pressed
1/2 teaspoon sugar
1/4 teaspoon ground ginger

Toss string beans in a large pot of boiling, heavily salted water. Bring water back to the boil and cook beans for 5 minutes. Pour into a colander and rinse under cold water; drain well. Place string beans in a shallow bowl.
Combine remaining ingredients and pour over string beans. Marinate for at least one hour, tossing occasionally. Serve at room temperature.

SERVES 4-6

Lemon Chicken

We like the zing of lemon in so many foods…it adds just enough snap to these chicken breasts.

3 whole chicken breasts, split, skinned, and boned
1 teaspoon salt
1/2 tablespoon fresh ground pepper
1 cup flour
3 to 4 tablespoons butter
2 cloves garlic, sliced
1 whole lemon, thinly sliced
Juice of 1 fresh lemon

Wash and pat dry chicken breasts.
Blend salt, pepper, and flour in a shallow bowl, and lightly dredge chicken.
Over a medium flame, heat the butter in a skillet. Sauté the sliced garlic until it is golden, then discard. Add the chicken breasts to the skillet and sauté for 6 to 8 minutes on each side, until golden brown. Add the lemon juice and continue cooking for 1 minute.
Remove chicken and put on warm serving platter, or individual plates. Garnish with two thin slices of lemon on each chicken breast. This also makes a good cold entrée.

SERVES 6

Gold Cornbread Fillets

Even non-fish eaters and kids like these crunchy, easy fish fillets. Spice and dress up with Charley's Chunky Tomato Sauce (see page 172).

3 large lemon sole fillets
³/4 cup balsamic vinegar
1 cup yellow cornmeal
¹/2 cup flour
¹/2 teaspoon salt
1 teaspoon pepper
4 tablespoons butter, melted
1 lemon, thinly sliced for garnish

Preheat oven to 450°.
Cut fillets into 2-inch strips across the width. Place in a shallow bowl and marinate in balsamic vinegar for about 10 minutes.
Combine dry ingredients on a platter. Shake excess vinegar off fillets and coat each strip with flour mixture. Place strips on an ungreased jelly roll pan, and drizzle over them melted butter. Bake at 450° for 20 minutes, or until golden. Garnish with thin lemon slices, and serve. (These may be eaten hot or cold.)

SERVES 6

Grilled Japanese Shrimp

Shrimp with a tangy, slightly Japanese flavor.

3 to 4 large shrimp per person (depending on size)
Tuna marinade plus 3 heaping tablespoons brown sugar and
  juice of 1 orange (see page 181)

Peel and devein shrimp, leaving tails on. Prepare the marinade. Marinate shrimp in a shallow glass platter for 1 hour, covered, in the refrigerator. Grill on a hibachi, outdoor grill, or under the broiler about 5 minutes per side, depending on size. Serve at once, using remaining marinade as dip at the table.

MAKES ENOUGH MARINADE FOR UP TO 6 SERVINGS OF SHRIMP

Charley's Drunken Shrimp

An elegant first course.

16 super-large shrimp
2 cloves garlic, minced
¹/2 cup olive oil
1 large onion
Salt and pepper to taste
Juice of ¹/2 lemon
1 lemon, seeded and thinly sliced
¹/2 cup dry white wine

Peel and devein shrimp, leaving the tails on. In a large skillet sauté the garlic in the olive oil for 2 minutes. Add the sliced onion and salt and pepper. Sauté until the onions become transparent. Add shrimp and sauté for 5 minutes, stirring to cook shrimp evenly. Add lemon juice, the lemon slices, and white wine, and cook for 3 to 4 minutes.
Remove from skillet and let cool to room temperature. Arrange shrimp artfully on a serving platter or on individual plates.

SERVES 4

Note: The shrimp may be refrigerated overnight. Bring back to room temperature before serving.

Grilled Fresh Tuna

If you have never tasted fresh tuna, this will be a real treat …it is nothing like the canned variety.

3/4-inch tuna steaks (1/2 pound per person)
2 tablespoons finely minced fresh ginger
2 teaspoons finely minced fresh garlic
2 teaspoons lemon zest
1/4 cup soy sauce
3/4 cup white wine

Combine all ingredients in a shallow glass or china platter. Marinate tuna for 1 hour, turning several times (do not refrigerate). Grill on a hibachi, outdoor grill, or under the broiler for 5 to 7 minutes per side, basting with marinade. Do not overcook, for a slightly undercooked center is best with fresh tuna.

MAKES ENOUGH MARINADE FOR UP TO 6 TUNA STEAKS

Zesty Bosc Pears

Poached fruit is delicious, and once made, there is always a ready supply on hand. This recipe for Bosc pears serves as the master instruction for the other poached pear, orange, and apple desserts that follow.

6 whole, firm Bosc pears
2 cups sweet sherry
1 cup light corn syrup
1 piece star anise, available in Oriental food stores (optional)
1 1 1/2-inch piece vanilla bean
1/4 cup each of lemon, orange, and lime peel strips
Fresh mint leaves for garnish

Wash and peel pears. Leave stems intact. In a stainless steel, enamelware, or glass pot large enough to hold a single layer of fruit, combine sherry, corn syrup, anise, vanilla bean, and citrus peel. Bring to a boil. Add fruit. Simmer, uncovered, until just softened but not mushy, or about ten to fifteen minutes. Do not overcook.

Remove from heat and let cool. Store, covered in poaching liquid, in tightly covered container in refrigerator until ready to serve. Keeps for several weeks. To serve, transfer fruit to decorative glass serving dish and spoon on liquid. Garnish with mint leaves.

SERVES 6

Seckel Pears Almondine

1 cup light corn syrup
1 cup water
1 cup Amaretto liqueur
1 1/2 pieces crystallized ginger, thinly sliced
About 12 Seckel pears (a tiny variety), scrubbed and unpeeled
1/4 cup sliced almonds for garnish

Combine corn syrup, water, liqueur, and ginger, and bring to a boil. Continue with poaching instructions for Bosc pear recipe. To serve, garnish with almonds.

SERVES 6

Oranges in Port Wine

3 cups tawny port
1 cinnamon stick
¹/₂ teaspoon juniper berries
¹/₂ teaspoon whole cloves
6 peeled navel oranges

Combine port and spices and bring to a boil. Add fruit and continue with poaching instructions for Bosc pear recipe.

SERVES 6

Cranberry/Maple Apples

1 12-ounce bottle maple-flavored syrup
1 cup light corn syrup
¹/₄ cup cranberry-flavored liqueur or juice
¹/₂ teaspoon whole allspice
6 firm, tart, peeled cooking apples, stems intact

Combine syrups, cranberry liqueur, and allspice, and bring to a boil. Continue with poaching instructions for Bosc pear recipe.

SERVES 6

Pears with Stilton Cores

Cheese and fruit all in one, and very pretty. Be certain to buy firm, beautiful pears with stems, preferably a little underripe.

6 Bosc pears (1 per person)
Juice of ½ lemon
½ pound Stilton cheese, at room temperature

With apple corer, core pears working from the bottom almost up to the stem. Stop coring about ½ inch from stem and twist core free. Remove core and immediately sprinkle inside of pears with lemon juice.

Cut a wedge of cheese a little larger than core, and then, using your fingers, push the cheese firmly into the pears. Wrap in plastic wrap and refrigerate until the cheese is firm, about 1½ hours.

When ready to serve, slice each pear crosswise into ¼-inch circles, then reassemble on individual plates.

SERVES 6

The Silver Palate's Lime Mousse

Tart and buttery lime mousse has been one of the Silver Palate's most popular desserts for years.

8 tablespoons (1 stick) sweet butter
5 eggs
1 cup granulated sugar
¾ cup fresh lime juice (6 or 7 limes)
Grated zest of 5 limes
2 cups heavy cream, chilled

Melt the butter in the top of a double boiler over simmering water. Beat eggs and sugar in a bowl until light and foamy. Slowly add mixture to melted butter, stirring constantly. Cook gently until mixture becomes a custard, about 10 minutes (do not overcook or eggs will scramble). Remove custard from heat and stir in the lime juice and grated zest. Cool to room temperature.

This step is unorthodox but crucial. Using an electric mixer, whip chilled cream until very stiff—almost, but not quite, to the point where it would become butter. Fold lime custard into whipped cream until just blended. Pour into 8 individual pots de crème, wineglasses, or goblets.

SERVES 8

The Silver Palate's Grand Marnier Chocolate Mousse

A fabulous experience for anyone who adores chocolate.

1 1/2 pounds semisweet chocolate chips
1/2 cup prepared espresso coffee
1/2 cup Grand Marnier
4 egg yolks
2 cups heavy cream, chilled
1/4 cup granulated sugar
8 egg whites
Pinch of salt
1/2 teaspoon vanilla extract
Candied rosebuds for garnish (optional)

Melt chocolate chips in a heavy saucepan over very low heat, stirring; add the espresso, then stir in the Grand Marnier. Let cool to room temperature. Add egg yolks, one at a time, beating thoroughly after each addition.

Whip 1 cup of the cream until thickened, then gradually add in the sugar, beating until stiff. Beat egg whites with salt until stiff. Gently fold egg whites into cream.

Stir about one third of cream and egg white mixture thoroughly into the chocolate. Then scrape remaining cream and egg mixture over lightened chocolate base and fold gently. Pour into 8 individual dessert cups or a serving bowl. Refrigerate for 2 hours, or until set.

At serving time, whip remaining cup of cream until thickened, add vanilla and whip to soft peaks. Top each portion of the mousse with a share of the cream and the candied rosebuds, if desired.

SERVES 8

Miss Remy's Madeleines

The "extraordinary thing" that happened to Proust happens to everyone who tastes these fabulous madeleines. We had a fantastic response to Miss Remy's madeleines at Wolfman • Gold & Good Company. If you can keep from eating them yourself, they make a wonderful gift.

4 whole eggs, extra large
1 egg yolk
1 1/2 cups fine sugar
1 teaspoon vanilla extract
1 1/2 teaspoons lemon zest
1 teaspoon orange zest
2 cups flour, sifted
1 1/2 cups clarified butter
Confectioners' sugar

Preheat oven to 375°. Using a small pastry brush, grease madeleine molds. Combine eggs, sugar, and vanilla in a large bowl, and heat over hot water. When the eggs are warm, remove from heat and beat in a mixer at *high* speed for about 15 minutes until the eggs are light and fluffy. They should triple in bulk. Fold the flour and lemon and orange zest into the eggs, then fold in the clarified butter. Spoon rounded tablespoons of the batter into the greased molds. Bake at 375° for 7 to 10 minutes, or until the tops are golden brown. Let the madeleines cool, then sprinkle lightly with confectioners' sugar.

MAKES 4 DOZEN MADELEINES

Note: Tightly covered, the madeleines will keep for up to two weeks. The longer they sit, the better they are with tea or coffee.

Eli Zabar's Shortbread Cookies

These shortbread cookies are even more of a treat when cut into heart shapes.

3/4 cup butter, at room temperature
1/2 cup sugar
1/2 teaspoon vanilla extract
1 3/4 cups flour
Pinch of salt

Cream the butter and sugar until well mixed, then blend in the vanilla extract. Add some salt to the flour, then combine flour and butter mixture. Refrigerate, after mixing, for 30 minutes.
Roll out chilled dough to 1/2-inch-thick sheet. Cut heart-shaped sections from the dough, and place them on silicone baking paper on a cookie sheet. Bake at 350° for about 20 minutes, or until cookies are light brown.

MAKES APPROXIMATELY 24 COOKIES

Chocolate Brownies in Doilies

The pretty lacy edge of paper doilies makes these gooey brownies real party fare.

2 sticks (1 cup) lightly salted butter
3 squares bitter chocolate
2 cups sugar
4 eggs, beaten
Pinch of salt
2 teaspoons vanilla extract
1 2/3 cups flour
Confectioners' sugar
6-inch paper doilies

In top of double boiler, melt butter and chocolate. Cool slightly. Whisk in sugar, then eggs, salt, and vanilla. Mix well. Stir in flour.
With fingertips press each paper doily into the well of an ungreased muffin tin. Using a ladle, fill halfway with brownie mixture, doing one at a time (the weight of the mixture will hold the doily "cup" in place). Be careful not to drip mixture on the lacy edge of doily. Bake at 350° for about 30 minutes on center rack, until done. Cool. Sprinkle with confectioners' sugar.

MAKES 16-18 BROWNIES

Peri's Lemon Squares

This is our favorite sweet to serve with a fresh fruit dessert.

¹/₂ cup butter (1 stick), at room temperature
1 cup all-purpose flour
¹/₄ cup confectioners' sugar
A pinch of salt

LEMON TOPPING:

2 eggs
1 cup granulated sugar
¹/₄ teaspoon salt
Juice and zest of 1 lemon
¹/₄ cup flour
¹/₂ teaspoon baking powder

Heat oven to 350°. In a food processor cream together the first four ingredients, until they form a ball.

With your fingers press the dough onto the bottom of a lightly buttered 8-inch baking pan.

Bake for 20 minutes. While the square is baking, prepare the lemon topping.

Beat eggs well, gradually adding the sugar. While continuing to beat the eggs and sugar, slowly add the remaining ingredients. Reduce oven to 325°. Pour the topping over the hot, baked shortbread, and return to the oven at once. Bake for 30 to 35 minutes, until the top is light gold. Remove the pan and run a sharp knife around the edges of the square. Cool for about 20 minutes, cut into squares, remove from pan, and arrange on a pretty serving plate or cake stand. Sprinkle with confectioners' sugar.

MAKES 9 SQUARES

4th of July Cake

Most people have a favorite white or yellow cake recipe, so use yours for this 4th of July cake. The art of this dessert lies in the decorating and the berries.

Double recipe for layer cake
2 pints heavy cream
1 tablespoon confectioners' sugar
1 teaspoon vanilla extract
2 pints strawberries
1 pint blueberries

Grease and flour a 17-by-12-by-½-inch roasting pan. Make up your cake recipe and pour into pan. So that you get a flat top cake, spread batter a little higher on sides and lower in the middle. Bake for 50 minutes at 350°. Test center for doneness with a toothpick. If it comes out clean, remove cake from oven. If center is still moist, bake 5 minutes longer and test again. When cake is done, run a knife around the edges and let cake cool.

Whip cream just until it starts to thicken. Add the confectioners' sugar and vanilla. Continue beating until the cream forms soft peaks. When cake is cool, pour all of the whipped cream on top and spread so that the cream covers the top of the cake.

Rinse, core, and slice strawberries in half vertically, then blot on paper towel. Rinse blueberries and pour onto paper towel to dry. With a knife, mark a rectangle in the upper left corner 6 inches long by 5½ inches wide and fill with blueberries. To form stripes with the sliced strawberries, start at the top of the cake next to the blueberries. Make 2 rows very close to each other. Then across the bottom of the cake make another 2 rows of strawberries. Do a third double row in the center of the cake, starting under the blueberries. For a touch of whimsy, place one whole strawberry with stem at the end of the final row.

SERVES 24

Almond Crunch

A crunchy candy-like topping for ice cream that is quick and easy, yet elegant when served in stemmed goblets.

2 tablespoons butter
1 cup slivered almonds
1/4 cup brown sugar

In a heavy skillet, melt butter until bubbly. Add the almonds and sauté until toasty brown. Add brown sugar and continue to cook until sugar is melted (about 2 minutes). Spoon hot over coffee or vanilla ice cream. Serve at once.

SERVES 6

Mimosa

Nothing could be simpler or more stylish than a mimosa at a Sunday brunch. To make an excellent one only requires the best ingredients.

1 quart freshly squeezed orange juice
1 bottle of your favorite champagne
1 orange, sliced

Use large balloon or tulip wineglasses. Fill about 1/3 full with orange juice. Place a slice of orange on the rim of each glass. When ready to serve, top off with champagne.

SERVES 6

Bellini

This is a classic at Harry's Bar in Venice. It is a wonderful brunch drink, or summer aperitif.

4 ripe peaches
1 bottle of champagne

Peel and slice the ripe peaches into the bowl of a food processor. Blend for about 1 minute.
Place a generous tablespoon of peach purée in the bottom of an oversized balloon wineglass. When ready to serve, pop the cork on a chilled bottle of your favorite champagne and fill the glasses halfway. Give one stir to combine. Saluti!

SERVES 6

White Wine Sangria

A lighter version of the traditional red sangria.

1 bottle of dry white wine
Juice of 2 oranges
1 orange, thinly sliced
1 lime, thinly sliced
1 lemon, thinly sliced
1 peach, peeled and sliced
1/4 cup extra-fine sugar
Club soda

Combine all ingredients except the club soda in a large glass pitcher. Stir. Refrigerate until ready to serve. When ready to serve, fill large wineglasses halfway, spooning several pieces of fruit into each. Add ice and top with club soda.

SERVES 6

A List of Recipes

Directory of Stores

The Directory of Stores is a guide to resources which can help enrich your own personal table-setting style. The list was carefully culled from friends, customers, magazine editors, and manufacturers. Each of these stores has replied to our questionnaire to help you best determine which stores most specifically fit your needs. Although we are not personally acquainted with all of the stores, we know them by reputation, and feel that each one has something special to offer.

Most of the shops listed are in the small to medium-size range. We have not listed many department stores as you would most likely be familiar with those in your area.

Hotel and restaurant merchandise is usually sold through distributors. Some distributors will sell directly to you if you know what you want, can buy at least a case of an item, make a decision on the spot, and pay cash. Look in your Yellow Pages for a distributor in your area.

Do not forget hardware and housewares stores, as well as the good old-fashioned 5 & 10s, for basics.

NOTE: Listings are alphabetized by first letter of business name.

ARIZONA

By George
7051 Fifth Avenue
Scottsdale 85251
(602) 994-1244

Table linens, baskets, paper goods, cookware, and cookbooks.

C. Steele
7303 East Indian School Road
Scottsdale 85251
(602) 994-4180

and

909 East Camelback Road
Phoenix 85018
(602) 234-1975

Imported pottery, baskets, china and glassware, country tablecloths, gourmet foods, wine, and cheese.

Cook's Bazaar
4424 East Camelback Road
Phoenix 85018
(602) 840-6793

Gourmet cookware and foods, cookbooks.

Duck and Decanter
1651 East Camelback Road
Phoenix 85018
(602) 274-5429

Kitchenware, baskets, cookbooks, coffees, teas, wines.

The Impeccable Pig
7042 East Indian School Road
Scottsdale 85251
(602) 941-1141

Antique and contemporary tableware, gourmet foods.

ARKANSAS

M.M. Cohn Co.
510 Main
Little Rock 72203
(501) 374-3311

Cookware, serving pieces, glassware, linens, candles.

NORTHERN CALIFORNIA

American Pie
3101 Sacramento Street
San Francisco 94115
(415) 929-8025

and

1 Ecker Street
San Francisco 94105
(415) 546-6040

Country pine furniture, American baskets, candles, gourmet foods, glassware, picnic ware, white dinnerware.

Caravansary
310 Sutter Street
San Francisco 94108
(415) 362-4641

and

2263 Chestnut Street
San Francisco 94123
(415) 921-3466

and

2908 College Avenue
Berkeley 94705
(415) 841-1628

and

230 Strawberry Town & Country
Mill Valley 94941
(415) 383-4161

*Restaurant-cum-retail store specializing in
cookware, linens, glassware, baskets, cookbooks,
picnic ware, food, and wine.*

Dandelion
2877 California Street
San Francisco 94115
(415) 563-3100

*Cookbooks, paper goods, food, candles, baskets,
glassware, and linens.*

Forrest Jones
3274 Sacramento Street
San Francisco 94115
(415) 567-2483

and

151 Jackson Street
San Francisco 94111
(415) 982-1577

*Gourmet cookware, baskets, dinnerware,
linens, trompe l'oeil bowls and platters.*

Grand Design
110 Serramonte Center
Daly City 94015
(415) 992-0885

and

166 Hillside Mall
San Mateo 94403
(415) 570-5510

*Contemporary, colorful housewares including
dinnerware, cookware, linens, flatware,
glassware, baskets, picnic ware, and candles.*

Grebitus & Son
1001 K Street
Country Club Center
Sacramento 95814
(916) 442-9081

*Antique silver, white china, crystal, flatware,
linens.*

Gump's
250 Post Street
San Francisco 94108
(415) 982-1616

*Excellent selection of china, crystal, flatware,
linens, cookware; specializing in Oriental
antiques.*

I. Magnin
Union Square
San Francisco 94108
(415) 362-2100

*Contemporary and traditional tableware,
baskets, linens, cookbooks.*

Judith-Ets Hokin Culinary Co.
3525 California Street
San Francisco 94118
(415) 668-3191

*Cooking school and store specializing in
professional cookware, food, whiteware, linens,
cookbooks.*

La Remise du Soleil
883 Sutter Street
San Francisco 94102
(415) 398-8646

*Unique selection of antique French country
furniture: armoires, tables, chairs, sideboards,
and accessories.*

La Ville du Soleil
556 Sutter Street
San Francisco 94102
(415) 434-0657

*Unique selection of antique and reproduction
French country tableware, baskets, linens,
glassware, hand-painted crockery, faience
animals.*

Macy's
170 O'Farrell
San Francisco 94102
(415) 397-3333

*Everything for the kitchen and the tabletop
including gourmet foods and cookware, tableware and linens, baskets, candles, picnic ware.*

Norman Shepherd, Inc.
458 Jackson Street
San Francisco 94111
(415) 362-4145

*17th-, 18th-, and 19th-century English and
continental tables, chairs, sideboards; Oriental
porcelains.*

Oakville Grocery
7856 St. Helena Highway
Oakville 94562
(707) 944-8802

Gourmet shop with baskets.

Regina Linens
3369 Sacramento Street
San Francisco 94118
(415) 563-8158

Formal contemporary and antique table linens.

Ronald James
3415 Sacramento Street
San Francisco 94118
(415) 567-7888

*Excellent selection of fine china; antique
tableware, flatware, glassware, linens.*

Sign of the Bear
435 First Street West
Sonoma 95476
(707) 996-3722

*A country store with tableware and
kitchenware.*

Sue Fisher King
3075 Sacramento Street
San Francisco 94115
(415) 922-7276

Italian pottery, linens, and terra-cotta.

Thomas A. Cara, Ltd.
317 Pacific Avenue
San Francisco 94133
(415) 781-0383

Large selection of espresso machines and professional cookware.

Tiffany & Co.
252 Grant Avenue
San Francisco 94108
(415) 781-7000

Fine selection of china, crystal, sterling flatware, table accessories.

Vivande/Porta Via
2125 Fillmore Street
San Francisco 94115
(415) 346-4430

Gourmet picnic baskets, imported foods, cookbooks.

Williams-Sonoma
576 Sutter Street
San Francisco 94102
(415) 982-0295

International collection of cookware, kitchenware, tableware, and gourmet foods.

SOUTHERN CALIFORNIA

The Brass Tree
9044 Burton Way
Beverly Hills 90211
(213) 276-1171

Antique furniture, porcelain and copper bakeware, baskets, damask linens, flatware, glassware, white dinnerware, wines.

Bullock's
7th and Hill Street

Los Angeles 90046
(213) 486-5603

Dinnerware, including oversized buffet plates and animal tureens; kitchenware, baskets, candles, oversized napkins.

Gazebo
8264 Melrose Avenue
Los Angeles 90046
(213) 658-7110

18th- and 19th-century English pine furniture; old and new imported and domestic baskets.

Geary's
351 North Beverly Drive
Beverly Hills 90210
(213) 273-4741/(800) 421-0566

China, crystal, silver, linens, cookware.

Gump's
9560 Wilshire Boulevard
Beverly Hills 90212
(213) 278-3200

Excellent selection of china, crystal, flatware, linens, cookware; specializing in Oriental antiques.

Linens, Etc.
16336 Ventura Boulevard
Encino 91436
(818) 995-8018

Odd-size and custom-made linens, candles, baskets, picnic ware, some French dinnerware.

Montana Mercantile
1324 Montana Avenue
Santa Monica 90403
(213) 451-1418

Contemporary, European-style cookware and tableware.

Port O'Call
906 Granite Drive
Pasadena 91101
(818) 796-7113

Baccarat crystal, Christofle silver, fine china, English place mats, pottery, antique tableware.

Shaxted
350 North Camden Drive
Beverly Hills 90210
(213) 273-4320

Imported table linens and accessories.

Tiffany & Co.
9502 Wilshire Boulevard
Beverly Hills 90212
(213) 273-8880

Fine selection of china, crystal, sterling flatware, table accessories.

COLORADO

A Place on Earth
141 East Meadow Drive
Vail 81657
(303) 476-1118

American artisan handcrafted table accessories.

Annie's
100 East Meadow Drive
Vail 81657
(303) 476-4197

Baccarat crystal, Christofle flatware, fine china, baskets, cookbooks.

The Best of All Worlds
300 Fillmore Street
Denver 80206
(303) 322-5968

French country faience dinnerware; cookware; baskets and linens.

International Villa
262 Fillmore Street
Denver 80206
(303) 333-1524

Baccarat and Lalique crystal, sterling flatware, fine traditional china.

Krismar
195 Goor Creek Drive
Vail 81658
(303) 476-3603

Traditional tableware.

Krismar
465 West Lionsthead Mall
Vail 81658
(303) 476-3603

Kitchenware and cookware.

CONNECTICUT

A Touch of Class
250 Greenwich Avenue
Greenwich 06830
(203) 869-6545

Traditional china and crystal; antique accessories.

British Country Antiques
50 Main Street North
Woodbury 06798
(203) 263-5100

Antique plate racks and furniture, earthenware and stoneware serving dishes, wood and metal kitchenware, baskets.

Church Street Trading Company
19 Church Street
New Milford 06776
(203) 355-2790

Country pottery, French bistro ware, handwoven rugs, willow furniture.

Cook's Bazaar
400 Crown Street
New Haven 06511
(203) 865-5088

Contemporary cookware and tableware; gourmet foods.

Hay Day
1050 East Putnam
Greenwich 06878
(203) 637-7600

and

1026 Post Road East
Westport 06880
(203) 227-9008

Country market including tableware, kitchenware, gourmet foods.

Lynnens, Inc.
The Village Square
115 Mason Street
Greenwich 06830
(203) 629-3659

Custom-made linens: Porthault, Pratesi, and Madeira linens.

Quimper Faience
141 Water Street
Stonington 06378
(203) 535-1712

The only store in the country devoted exclusively to the French provincial hand-painted earthenware of Quimper, France.

The Seraph
Goodspeed Landing
East Haddam 06423
(203) 873-8381

Bistro flatware, Porcelaine d'Auteuil, blue Canton china, cookware, baskets.

The Silo
Upland Road
New Milford 06776
(203) 355-0300

Food, kitchenware, picnic baskets.

The Write Approach
1314 Whalley Avenue
New Haven 06515
(203) 397-8272

Hand-loomed place mats and napkins, baskets, antique fish sets, hand-painted Portuguese platters, gourmet foods, cookbooks.

DISTRICT OF COLUMBIA

Cherishables
1068 20th Street, N.W.
Washington 20009
(202) 785-4087

18th- and 19th-century American country furniture and accessories; contemporary cottons; baskets; porcelain.

Cornelia Wickens Liberty
1513 Wisconsin Avenue, N.W.
Washington 20007
(202) 337-5742

Hand-painted dinnerware, antique linens, baskets.

Kitchen Bazaar
4455 Connecticut Avenue, N.W.
Washington 20008
(202) 244-1550

International cookware and dinnerware; spices, baskets, picnic ware.

FLORIDA

Basketville
4011 S. Tamiami Trail
Venice 33595
(813) 493-0007

Baskets, buckets, pottery, wooden utensils, rustic place mats and napkins.

Bedfellow's
3425 Thomasville Road
Tallahassee 32308
(904) 893-1713

Formal place mats and napkins, French jacquard linens.

Carani
150 Worth Avenue
Palm Beach 33480
(305) 655-6462

Handmade ceramic objects for the table.

The Cookshop
7251 S.W. 96th Street
Miami 33143
(305) 667-5957

Food, cookware, cookbooks, baskets.

Kassatlys
238 Worth Avenue
Palm Beach 33480
(305) 655-5665

Custom-made tablecloths and place mats; ready-made European table linens.

Melangerie II
150 Worth Avenue
Palm Beach 33480
(305) 659-5119

Old lace, tea services, fruit compotes, caviar servers, toast racks, porcelain breakfast sets from England.

Nessa Gaulois
9700 Collins Avenue
Bal Harbour 33154
(305) 864-3226
and
3390 Mary Street
Coconut Grove 33133
(305) 448-7391

China, crystal, flatware, linens, French stainless steel cookware.

Our Warehouse
301 Northeast 36th Street
Oakland Park 33334
(305) 565-2867

Restaurant supply dinnerware and foods, including Villeroy and Boch china, Porcelaine d'Auteuil, Reidel and Orrefors glassware, a selection of 800 wines, caviars, imported cheeses.

The Unpressured Cooker
32 Periwinkle Place
Sanibel 33957
(813) 472-2413

Calphalon and Le Creuset cookware; cookbooks.

GEORGIA

Tabby House
105 Retreat Street
St. Simons Island 31522
(912) 638-2257

Handmade wreaths and baskets, antique serving ware; cookbooks.

Tiffany & Co.
Phipps Plaza
3500 Peachtree Road, N.E.
Atlanta 30326
(404) 261-0075

Fine selection of china, crystal, sterling flatware, table accessories.

ILLINOIS

Art Mart/Art Mart Foods
127 Lincoln Square
Urbana 61801
(217) 344-7979

Food, kitchenware, dinnerware, linens.

City
213 Institute Place
Chicago 60610
(312) 664-9581

Contemporary housewares.

Complete Accessories
554 Lincoln Avenue
Winnetka 60093
(312) 441-6747

Contemporary tableware including handmade ceramics and baskets.

Country Shop
710 Oak Street
Winnetka 60093
(313) 441-8690

Antique tables and chairs, linens, slipware and salt-glaze tableware.

Crate and Barrel
850 North Michigan Avenue
Chicago 60611
(312) 787-5900

Contemporary cookware, glassware, and tableware.

Handle with Care
1706 North Wells
Chicago 60614
(312) 751-2929

French serving ware, French jacquard linens, stoneware.

Material Possessions
954 Green Bay Road
Winnetka 60093
(312) 446-8840

Hand-painted table linens, handmade glassware, dinnerware, and ceramics.

Panache et Cie, Ltd.
714 Vernon Avenue
Glencoe 60022
(312) 835-0030

Dinnerware, glassware, flatware, linens, baskets, candles.

Private Lives
473 Roger Williams Avenue
Highland Park 60035
(312) 432-2000

Custom-made table linens.

Tiffany & Co.
715 North Michigan Avenue
Chicago 60611
(312) 944-7500

Fine selection of china, crystal, sterling flatware, table accessories.

Top Brass
337 Park Avenue

Glencoe 60022
(312) 835-0690

Table linens, kitchenware, tableware.

INDIANA

Good's, Inc.
College Mall
Bloomington 47401
(812) 339-2200

Wedgewood and Spode china, flatware, crystal, linens, gourmet cookware, cookbooks, baskets.

Shop of John Simmons
8702 Keystone at the Crossing
Indianapolis 46240
(317) 846-4273

Kitchenware, cookbooks, crystal, flatware, china, linens.

IDAHO

Lynnens, Inc.
Ketchum 83340
(208) 726-3930

Custom-made linens; Porthault, Pratesi, and Madeira table linens.

IOWA

Duck Soup
116 South Market
Ottumwa 52501
(515) 682-9583

Country kitchenware, baskets, cookbooks, coffees, jams, and spices.

Egg Shell
205A Valley West Mall
West Des Moines 50265
(515) 223-5778

High-tech kitchenware.

Kitchen Tools
138 Fifth Street

West Des Moines 50265
(515) 277-8432

Cuisinart and Calphalon cookware, cutlery, kitchenware, cookbooks.

Kitchenworks
Lyndale Mall
Cedar Rapids 52502
(319) 393-0710

Functional kitchenware, cookware.

The Peppermill
Indian Hills Shopping Center
Sioux City 51104
(712) 255-9842

Tableware and kitchenware; cookbooks, baskets.

Things and Things and Things
130 South Clinton Street
Iowa City 52240
(319) 337-9641

Contemporary table accessories and linens; coffee makers and servers; gourmet foods; cookbooks.

KANSAS

Gourmet Corner
The Mall at Fifth
Atchison 66002
(913) 367-1086

Imported cheeses, coffees, teas; baskets; kitchenware.

The Paper Plate
4018 West 83rd Street
Prairie Village 66208
(913) 341-7701

Paper goods, plastic cutlery, cookbooks.

KENTUCKY

Maxwell House
380 South Mill Street
Lexington 40508
(606) 254-3954

Antique table accessories, traditional china, glassware and flatware, linens, baskets.

LOUISIANA

Coleman Adler's
722-24 Canal Street
New Orleans 70130
(504) 523-5292

Traditional and contemporary dinnerware; cookware.

Jay Aronson, Ltd.
200 Broadway
New Orleans 70118
(504) 865-1186

Traditional china, crystal, and silver.

Wok and Whisk
2295 Hollydale
Baton Rouge 70808
(504) 769-5122

Informal china and glassware, kitchenware, baskets, cookbooks.

MAINE

Howard and Mullen
Main Street
Ogunquit 03907
(207) 646-4098

Dinnerware and bakeware from the 1920s to the 1950s, including Fiesta, Harlequin, Franciscan china, and Chromium appliances.

Maine's Mass House
Route 1
Lincolnville 04849
(207) 789-5705

Contemporary dinnerware and kitchenware.

MARYLAND

The China Closet
6807 Wisconsin Avenue
Chevy Chase 20815
(301) 656-5400

Contemporary dinnerware, linens, cookbooks, gourmet cookware.

Kitchen Bazaar
Annapolis Mall
Annapolis 21401
(301) 224-4414

and

Towson Town Centre
Towson 21204
(301) 337-8900

and

Montgomery Mall
Bethesda 20814
(301) 365-5555

International cookware and dinnerware; spices, baskets, picnic ware.

Stebbins Anderson
802 Kenilworth Drive
Towson 21204
(301) 823-6600

Informal dishes, linens, kitchenware.

The Store, Ltd.
Village of Cross Keys
Baltimore 21210
(301) 323-2350

Contemporary tableware, cookware, baskets, ceramic crocks.

MASSACHUSETTS

Basketville
200 Hudson Street
Northboro 01532
(617) 393-2147

and

419 Main Street
Sturbridge 01566
(617) 347-3493

Baskets, buckets, pottery, wooden utensils, rustic place mats and napkins.

Cook's Nook
65 Mass. Avenue
Luneburg 01462
(617) 342-8727

French and Italian gourmet cookware; cookbooks; wicker bread baskets.

Crate and Barrel
Copley Place
100 Huntington Avenue
Boston 02116
(617) 536-9400

and

48 Brattle Street
Cambridge 02138
(617) 876-6300

Contemporary cookware, glassware, and tableware.

The Elegant Picnic
Stockbridge 01262
(413) 298-4010

Exceptional picnics made to order.

Fabrications
1740 Mass. Avenue
Cambridge 02138
(617) 661-6276

Contemporary table linens; bright contemporary dishes.

Kitchen Arts
161 Newbury Street
Boston 02116
(617) 266-8701

Cookware, cutlery, cookbooks, baskets.

The Lion's Paw
Main Street
Nantucket 02554
(617) 228-3827

Painted pottery, bed trays, traditional linens and housewares.

The Little Store
29 State Road

Great Barrington 01230
no phone

Antique ceramic and wood tableware; baskets.

O'Rama's
148 Washington Street
Marblehead 01945
(617) 631-0894

Antique and one-of-a-kind contemporary linens, dinnerware, baskets.

MICHIGAN

Artisan, Inc.
1122 South University
Ann Arbor 48104
(313) 662-5595

Contemporary tableware including Waterford and Spode; linens; cookware; candles.

Bowring Brothers
662 Briarwood Mall
Ann Arbor 48104
(313) 994-4428

Traditional to contemporary dinnerware, linens; oak tables and chairs, contemporary bistro sets.

Clancy's Place
200 Renaissance
Suite 226
Detroit 48243
(313) 259-6170

Cookware, dinnerware, linens, baskets, cookbooks.

Complete Cuisine, Ltd.
322 South Main Street
Ann Arbor 48104
(313) 662-0046

Foods, cookbooks, baskets, teapots, and table accessories.

Gattle's
Lake and Howard Streets
Petosky 49770
(616) 347-3982

Table linens.

Horn of Plenty
422 South Woodward
Birmingham 48011
(313) 645-2750

*Contemporary dinnerware, stainless flatware,
glasses, baskets, cookware, linens.*

John Leidy Shop
607 East Liberty
Ann Arbor 48108
(313) 668-6779

*Contemporary and traditional china,
stoneware, crystal, flatware, linens, cookware.*

Kitchen Glamour
26770 Grand River
Redford 48240
(313) 537-1300

Cookbooks and kitchenware.

Kitchen Port
415 North Fifth Avenue
Ann Arbor 48104
(313) 665-9188

*Cookware, kitchenware, dinnerware, baskets,
cookbooks.*

Orthogonality
135 South Woodward Avenue
Birmingham 48011
(313) 642-1460

*Cookware, dinnerware, casual linens, candles,
baskets.*

Seasons
518 Frandor
Lansing 48912
(517) 332-0897

*Casual furniture and dinnerware, paper goods
and plastic cutlery, candles, baskets, cookbooks.*

MINNESOTA

Cinnamon Toast
3940 West 50th Street

Edina 55424
(612) 920-4070
and
1603 Plymouth Road
Minnetonka 55343
(612) 545-2130
and
327 Rosedale Center
Roseville 55113
(612) 545-2148

Contemporary cookware, baskets, paper goods.

Dayton's
700 on the Mall
Minneapolis 55343
(612) 375-3000

*White dinnerware, glassware, casual table
linens, cookware, flatware, cookbooks.*

Five Swans
309 East Lake Street
Wayzata 55391
(612) 473-4685

*Dinnerware, cookware, linens, paper goods,
picnic ware.*

Provisions
3421 Hazleton Road
Edina 55435
(612) 474-6953

Gourmet kitchenware.

Provisions
320 Water Street
Excelsior 55331
(612) 474-6953

*Baskets, casual table linens, paper goods,
cookbooks, candles, white dinnerware.*

MISSOURI

Halls Crown Center
25th and Grand Avenue
Kansas City 64108
(816) 274-8111

Contemporary kitchenware.

Halls Plaza
211 Nichols Road
Kansas City 64112
(816) 274-3322

Traditional china, crystal, flatware.

Pampered Pantry
8139 Maryland Avenue
St. Louis 63105
(314) 727-5088

*Gourmet cookware and foods, cookbooks,
casual linens.*

Superlatives
Country Club Plaza
234 Nichols Road
Kansas City 64112
(816) 561-7610

*Antiques including tables and chairs, bowls
and serving platters, silver, ceramic toast racks.*

NEBRASKA

Table Manners
10914 Elm Street
Omaha 68144
(402) 392-0667

Dinnerware, table linens, candles.

NEW JERSEY

Dining Inn
2 West Northfield Road
Livingston 07039
(201) 992-8300

American handcrafted pottery, glass, baskets.

Eagle's Nest
Country Mile Route 202
Morristown 07960
(201) 766-1372

*Traditional and antique china, gourmet food,
Pierre Deux linens, baskets.*

Expressions Unlimited
165 Washington Valley Road

Warren 07060
(201) 469-6969

Gourmet food, kitchenware, picnic baskets and accessories, cookbooks, candles.

Platypus
233 Route 18
East Brunswick 08816
(201) 846-1333

Tableware, kitchenware, gourmet food, baskets.

Table of Contents
12 Sylvan Avenue
Englewood Cliffs 07632
(201) 944-2155

Traditional and contemporary china, crystal, place mats, and accessories.

Settings
506 Millburn Avenue
Short Hills 07078
(201) 379-5666

Dinnerware, fine linens, cookware.

NEW MEXICO

Cookworks
316 Guadalupe Street
Santa Fe 87501
(505) 988-7676

Professional cookware, glassware, linens, dishes, baskets, picnic ware.

Design Warehouse
128 East Marcy
Santa Fe 87501
(505) 988-1555

Casual furniture, tableware, linens, and cookware.

Pennysmith's
4022 Rio Grande Boulevard, N.W.
Albuquerque 87107
(505) 345-2383

Paper goods, gourmet foods, baskets, contemporary dinnerware, cookware.

NEW YORK CITY

Ad Hoc Housewares
842 Lexington Avenue
New York 10022
(212) 752-5488

Functional contemporary cookware, glassware, and dinnerware.

Ad Hoc Softwares
410 West Broadway
New York 10012
(212) 925-2652

Contemporary natural fiber table linens.

The American Country Store
969 Lexington Avenue
New York 10021
(212) 744-6705

Country furniture and table accessories.

Anichini at Barney's
Seventh Avenue and 17th Street
New York 10011
(212) 929-9000

Antique table linens, lace, embroidery, damask.

Barney's Chelsea Passage
Seventh Avenue and 17th Street
New York 10011
(212) 929-9000

Excellent selection of antique and new china, flatware, crystal, baskets; imported dinnerware; French and Italian table linens.

Bergdorf Goodman
754 Fifth Avenue
New York 10019
(212) 753-7300

Antiques, dinnerware, European cookware, baskets, fine linens.

Bloomingdale's
1000 Third Avenue
New York 10022
(212) 355-5900

Huge and varied assortment of tableware, kitchenware, cookware, decorative accessories, candles, baskets, picnic ware.

Cherchez
864 Lexington Avenue
New York 10021
(212) 737-8215

Potpourri, fine antique linens, antique lace, and porcelain.

Conran's
The Market at Citicorp
160 East 54th Street
New York 10022
(212) 371-2225/(800) 431-2718

Simple, contemporary furniture, linens, dinnerware, glasses, flatware, cookware, candles, baskets, picnic accessories.

D.F. Sanders & Co.
386 West Broadway
New York 10012
(212) 925-9040
and
962 Madison Avenue
New York 10021
(212) 879-6161

High-tech tableware and housewares.

Dean & DeLuca
121 Prince Street
New York 10012
(212) 431-1691

European tableware and professional cookware, copper pots, and gourmet foods.

Descamps
723 Madison Avenue
New York 10021
(212) 355-2522

Imported French linens.

Elizabeth Eakins
1053 Lexington Avenue
New York 10021
(212) 628-1950

One-of-a-kind hand-woven custom-dyed rugs; patterned pottery buffet plates.

Gordon Foster, Ltd.
1322 Third Avenue
New York 10021
(212) 744-4922

Antique furniture and baskets; handmade pottery for the table.

H. Roth & Son
1577 First Avenue
New York 10023
(212) 734-1111

Bakeware, cookware, cookbooks, kitchenware, foods, herbs, coffees and teas; cake decorating classes.

Henri Bendel
10 West 57th Street
New York 10019
(212) 247-1100

Lee Bailey: up-to-the minute housewares and tablewares; Frank McIntosh: ever-changing assortment of table linens, contemporary flatware, glassware, accessories.

Howard Kaplan's French Country Store
35 East 10th Street
New York 10003
(212) 674-1000

French country antiques and reproductions.

James Robinson
15 East 57th Street
New York 10022
(212) 752-6166

Handmade sterling flatware and tea and coffee services; fine antique silver, porcelain, glass.

Jean Hoffman/Jana Starr Antiques
236 East 80th Street
New York 10021
(212) 861-8256

Antique table linens.

Jenny B. Goode
1194 Lexington Avenue
New York 10028
(212) 794-2492

Antique and contemporary cookware, baskets, candles, dinnerware, glassware, linens, table accessories.

Judi Boisson
4 East 82nd Street
New York 10028
(212) 734-5844
(by appointment only)

Antique American quilts; antique European linens.

La Cuisinière
968 Lexington Avenue
New York 10021
(212) 861-4475

Traditional and antique cookware and dinnerware; large platters.

Laura Ashley
818 Madison Avenue
New York 10021
(212) 517-3772

English country prints on china, crockery, napkins, and place mats; fabrics.

Macy's Cellar
Macy's Herald Square
New York 10001
(212) 695-4400

Excellent assortment of tableware, kitchenware, gourmet foods.

Marimekko
7 West 56th Street
New York 10019
(212) 581-9616

Contemporary linens and dinnerware; baskets, candles, antiques.

Maya Schaper Antiques
152 East 70th Street
New York 10021
(212) 734-9427

Antique flatware and table accessories; country linens.

Mayhew
509 Park Avenue
New York 10022
(212) 759-8120

Imported china, flatware, and glassware, casual furniture and linens.

Of All Things
900 First Avenue
New York 10022
(212) 752-3628

Dinnerware, paper goods, kitchenware, linens.

Of Kitchen Things
1144 Lexington Avenue
New York 10021
(212) 744-3372

Specializing in hand-painted dinnerware, ceramic serving pieces and coordinated linens; picnic baskets and accessories.

Pierre Deux Antiques
369 Bleecker Street
New York 10014
(212) 243-7740

Antiques, accessories, lamps, French faience tableware.

Pierre Deux
381 Bleecker Street
New York 10014
(212) 675-5054
and

870 Madison Avenue
New York 10021
(212) 570-9343

*Country French cotton table linens,
dinnerware, baskets, antiques.*

Pottery Barn
117 East 59th Street (main store)
New York 10022
(212) 741-9132

*Casual contemporary cookware, white
dinnerware, glassware, storage baskets and
jars, paper goods and picnic accessories.*

The Silver Palate
274 Columbus Avenue
New York 10023
(212) 799-6340

Gourmet food, picnic baskets, cookbooks.

Tiffany & Co.
727 Fifth Avenue
New York 10022
(212) 755-8000

*Fine selection of china, crystal, sterling
flatware, table accessories.*

Vito Giallo Antiques
966 Madison Avenue
New York 10021
(212) 535-9885

Antique china and objets d'art.

The Wicker Garden
1318 Madison Avenue
New York 10028
(212) 410-7000

*Antique wicker tables, chairs, high chairs,
trays, baskets; antique tablecloths and napkins.*

Wolfman·Gold & Good Company
484 Broome Street
New York, New York 10013
(212) 431-1888

and

142 East 73rd Street
New York 10021
(212) 288-0404

*Oversized white dinnerware and glassware,
French restaurant flatware, antique linens,
French, Italian, and Chinese napkins, baskets,
porcelain menu cards, paper doilies.*

Zabar's
2245 Broadway
New York 10024
(212) 787-2000

Gourmet foods; cookware and kitchenware.

NEW YORK STATE

Balasses House Antiques
Main Street & Hedges Lane
Amagansett 11930
(516) 267-3032

*18th- and 19th-century country tables, chairs,
armoires, buffets; earthenware platters, bowls,
dishes, glasses.*

C & W Mercantile
Main Street
Bridgehampton 11932
(516) 537-7914

*French and Swiss jacquard linens, rag and
dhurrie rugs, baskets, candles, picnic ware.*

Cliffhangers
66 Pondfield Road
Bronxville 10708
(914) 793-2397

*Doilies, baskets, dhurrie and rag rugs, Liberty
print fabrics, English pine tables and chairs,
folk art accessories, Portuguese soup tureens
and platters.*

Consider The Cook
Yellow Monkey Village
Cross River 10518
(914) 763-8844

*A country store with tableware, cookware,
linens, and cookbooks.*

Éclat
20 East Parkway
Scarsdale 10583
(914) 725-3525

*Contemporary tableware and kitchenware,
place mats, trays, baskets, cookbooks,
picnic ware.*

Engell Pottery
One Main Street
East Hampton 11937
(516) 324-6462

*International selection of baskets of all shapes
and sizes.*

The Gilded Carriage
95 Tinker Street
Woodstock 12498
(914) 679-2607

*Gourmet kitchenware, dinnerware, linens,
baskets, hand-painted Italian pottery,
paper doilies.*

Judi Boisson
28C Jobs Lane
Southampton 19968
(516) 283-5424

Wicker furniture, American antique quilts.

Kitchen Privileges
6 Bond Street
Great Neck 11021
(516) 466-4884

*Kitchenware, cookbooks, white dinnerware,
linens.*

Norman Shepherd Antiques
Montauk Highway
Water Mill 11976
(516) 726-4840

*18th-, 19th-, 20th-century English and
European furniture; Oriental porcelains.*

Old Acquaintance
Main Street
Bridgehampton 19932
(516) 537-0909

Antique tables, chairs, sideboards, armoires, table accessories.

Positively Main Street
773 Elmwood
Buffalo 14222
(716) 882-5858

Contemporary table accessories, baskets, serving pieces.

Prima Casa
508 Central Avenue
Cedarhurst 11516
(516) 295-1552

Signed, handcrafted dinnerware; baskets, candles, linens.

Private Collections
489 Central Avenue
Cedarhurst 11516
(516) 295-0779

English antique tables, sideboards, armoires; antique tableware and linens; picnic baskets and accessories, paper doilies.

Quogue Emporium, Ltd.
98 Riverhead Road
Westhampton Beach 11978
(516) 288-6262

Glassware, china, crystal, linens, baskets, rugs, candles, cookware, cookbooks.

Richard Camp Antiques
Montauk Highway
Wainscott 11975
(516) 537-0330

Stripped pine country furniture; china and flatware of many periods.

Tivoli Imports
27 Main Street
Southampton 11968
(516) 283-8307

Salad and dessert plates, glassware, cutlery, china baskets.

Tools of the Trade
Amagansett Square
Main Street
Amagansett 11930
(516) 267-6662

Contemporary tableware, cookware, picnic ware, and gadgets.

Yellow Monkey Village Antiques
Route 35
Cross River 10518
(914) 763-5848

Large selection of stripped pine tables, chairs, hutches, sideboards, and table accessories.

NORTH CAROLINA

Applegate and Company
127 Fourth Avenue West
Hendersonville 28739
(704) 697-7057

Contemporary European and American tableware; 19th-century English and American country furniture; baskets.

La Cache
217 Reynolds village
Winston-Salem 27106
(919) 727-1515

Traditional and contemporary china, crystal, and silver, place mats, antique and new table accessories.

M. Grodzicki & Co.
611 Providence Road
Charlotte 28207
(704) 334-7300

Antique majolica pottery, china, flatware, linens, doilies.

Masterpiece
Oak Spring Road
Rutherfordton 28139
(704) 287-3264

Brass table accessories, baskets.

NORTH DAKOTA

Creative Kitchen
West Acres
Fargo 58103
(701) 282-8694

Contemporary kitchenware including paper goods and cookbooks.

OHIO

A.B. Closson, Jr. Co.
401 Race Street
Cincinnati 45202
(513) 762-5519

Dinnerware, cookware, linens, cookbooks, picnic ware.

Common market
7811 Montgomery Road
Cincinnati 45236
(513) 793-2783

Contemporary tableware and cookware, baskets, cookbooks, coffees and teas.

Country Collections
109 South High Street
Dublin 43017
(614) 889-7772

Dinnerware, flatware, glassware, baskets, cookbooks, picnic ware.

Designer Warehouse
1677 West Lane
Columbus 43221
(614) 488-0793

Contemporary and traditional dinnerware, flatware, crystal, linens, baskets.

Gattle's
3456 Michigan Avenue
Cincinnati 45208
(513) 871-4050

Traditional table linens.

Giftique
7809 Montgomery Road
Cincinnati 45236
(513) 891-4100

Tableware, linens, baskets, paper goods.

The Place Settings East
5125 East Main Street
Columbus 43213
(614) 866-0684

Tableware and kitchenware, linens, picnic ware, paper goods.

Potter and Mellen
10405 Carnegie Avenue
Cleveland 44106
(216) 231-5100

English and French dinnerware, Baccarat crystal, antique and reproduction silver, gourmet cookware, linens.

Quailcrest Farm
2810 Armstrong Road
Wooster 44691
(216) 345-6722

Country stoneware, baskets, cookbooks, casual linens, paper goods and picnic baskets, fresh herbs and herb wreaths.

OKLAHOMA

Rack-N-Stack
Woodland Hills Mall
7021 South Memorial
Tulsa 74133
(918) 250-0476

Picnic ware and wire shelving.

OREGON

Cloudtree & Sun
112 North Main Street
Gresham 97030
(503) 666-8495

Gourmet cookware and tableware, fine linens, gourmet foods.

Kitchen Kaboodle
606 S.W. Washington
Portland 97205
(503) 227-5131

and

Progress Shopping Center
S.W. Hall Boulevard
Portland 97205
(503) 643-5491

Cookware, dinnerware, linens, baskets, cookbooks.

Le Paradis
2320 Northwest Westover Road
Portland 97210
(503) 222-4050

Imported linens.

PENNSYLVANIA

Basketville
Route 30
Paradise 17562
(717) 442-9444

Baskets, buckets, pottery, wooden utensils, rustic place mats and napkins.

Bon Appetit
213 South 17th Street
Philadelphia 19103
(215) 546-8059

Contemporary and country cookware; porcelain, glassware, cookbooks.

Chef's Bazaar
7 Central Plaza
Lancaster 17062
(717) 392-2295

Gourmet cookware, hand-thrown pottery, cutlery, linens.

Descamps
1733 Walnut Street
Philadelphia 19103
(215) 567-7886

Imported French linens.

Maison de Campagne
Freight House Shops
Station Square
Pittsburgh 15219
(412) 765-0587

Quimper and Luneville French dinnerware; French faience tureens, platters, serving pieces; imported French flatware.

Necessities, Ltd.
814 South Aiken Avenue
Pittsburgh 15232
(412) 621-5600

Linens imported from Italy, Ireland, Madeira.

RHODE ISLAND

Country Loft
3964 Main Road
Tiverton 02878
(401) 624-2142

Oak and pine tables and chairs, antique cupboards, high chairs, children's tables and chairs.

Rue De France
78 Thames Street
Newport 02840
(401) 846-2084

French cotton lace place mats and table runners.

SOUTH CAROLINA

Basketville
Highway 501
Myrtle Beach 29578
(803) 293-5555

Baskets, buckets, pottery, wooden utensils, rustic place mats and napkins.

SOUTH DAKOTA

Kitchen Connection
424 South Main

Aberdeen 57401
(605) 225-9566

Dinnerware, kitchenware, baskets, cookbooks.

Larsen Designs, Ltd.
1608 South Western Avenue
Sioux Falls 57105
(605) 336-6037

Paper goods, kitchenware, candles, baskets, coffees.

TENNESSEE

Linen Store
4045 Hillsboro Road
Nashville 37215
(615) 383-6062

Traditional china, glassware, table linens, baskets, cookware.

TEXAS

Colbert
2001 Wolfin Village
Amarillo 79108
(806) 353-5571

Formal and informal china, crystal, linens, kitchenware, baskets.

The Container Store
6060 Forest Lane
Dallas 75230
(214) 386-5054

and

3060 Mockingbird Lane
Dallas 75205
(214) 373-7044

and

6131 Campbell Road
Dallas 75248
(214) 248-0981

and

1522 North Collins
Lincoln Square Shopping Center

Arlington 76011
(214) 261-3388

Wire shelving.

Crate and Barrel
220 North Park Center
Dallas 75225
(214) 392-3411

Contemporary cookware, glassware, tableware.

drummonds
5345 Westheimer
Houston 77056
(713) 626-5090

Contemporary kitchenware and tableware.

East & Orient Company
2901 North Henderson Avenue
Dallas 75206
(214) 826-1191

Antique tableware and fine linens.

Gump's
The Houston Galleria
5051 Westheimer
Houston 77086
(713) 850-8600

and

13350 Dallas Parkway
Dallas 75240
(214) 392-0200

Excellent selection of china, crystal, flatware, linens, cookware; specializing in Oriental antiques.

The Gypsy Savage
3012 Phil Fall
Houston 77098
(713) 528-0897

Victorian and Edwardian table accessories; linens, baskets.

Jones and Jones
2100 South Tenth
McAllen 78503
(512) 687-1171

Tableware, kitchenware, linens, antiques, baskets, paper goods.

Piccadilly Fair
520 North Park Center
Dallas 75225
(214) 691-4459

Antique, formal, and informal linens; dinnerware, cookbooks, picnic ware.

Tiffany & Co.
The Dallas Galleria
13350 Dallas Parkway
Dallas 75240
(214) 458-2800

and

The Houston Galleria
5015 Westheimer
Houston 77056
(713) 626-0220

Fine selection of china, crystal, sterling flatware, table accessories.

Via Condotti
3214 Oak Lawn Avenue
Dallas 75219
(214) 559-2111

Imported and domestic dinnerware, antique table accessories, espresso pots, linens.

The Victorian Lady
All That's Lovely Antiques
Cole's Antique Village
1020 North Main
Pearland 77581
(713) 485-5244

Victorian lace and linen.

VERMONT

Basketville
RFD #1, Route 5
Putney 05346
(802) 387-4351

and

Historical Route 7
Arlington 05240
(802) 362-1609

Baskets, buckets, pottery, wooden utensils, rustic place mats and napkins.

F. H. Gillingham & Sons
16 Elm Street
Woodstock 05091
(802) 457-2100

100-year-old New England general store with everything from "caviar to manure."

Weston House
Route 100
Weston 05161
(802) 824-3010

American quilts and baskets.

VIRGINIA

Basketville
Route 60
Williamsburg 23168
(804) 564-3584

Baskets, buckets, pottery, wooden utensils, rustic place mats and napkins.

Full Circle
317 Cameron Street
Alexandria 22314
(703) 683-4500

Imported and hand-crafted dinnerware; cookware; linens.

June Kramer
1904 Colley Avenue
Norfolk 23517
(804) 625-1211

Country French antiques, European cookware, baskets.

Kitchen Bazaar
Seven Corners Shopping Center
Falls Church 22044
(703) 534-0220

International cookware and dinnerware; spices, baskets, picnic ware.

WASHINGTON

Domus
141 Bellevue Square
Bellevue 98004
(206) 454-2728

Contemporary dinnerware and table linens.

Magnolia Kitchen Shoppe
and Cooking School
2416-32 West
Seattle 98199
(206) 282-2665

Gourmet cookware, linens, dinnerware, cookbooks, coffees and teas.

Mr. "J" Kitchen Gourmet
10630 N.E. 8th
Bellevue 98004
(206) 455-2270

Cookware, dinnerware, linens, paper goods.

Opus
204 Broadway East
Seattle 98102
(206) 325-1781

Non-traditional white china, Italian glassware, antique textiles, baskets, Chinese fish plates and Chinese blue-and-white serving bowls, local handmade pottery.

Seattle Design Store
406 Broadway East
Seattle 98102
(206) 324-9700
and
2943 N.E. Blakely
Seattle 98105
(206) 523-7500
and
1619 Westlake Mall
Seattle 98101
(206) 625-0500

and
273 Bellevue Square
Bellevue 98004
(206) 455-4300

Contemporary tableware and cookware.

Sur La Table
84 Pine Street
Pike Place Farmer's Market
Seattle 98101
(206) 622-2459

Gourmet cookware, restaurant stemware and oversized dinnerware, French linens.

WISCONSIN

Percy's
719 North Milwaukee Street
Milwaukee 53202
(414) 271-4737

Custom-made table linens, china, crystal, cookbooks, table accessories.

Potpourri
2500 North Mayfair Road
Wawatosa 53226
(414) 475-0033

Contemporary stoneware, glassware, kitchenware, baskets, cookbooks.

Stock Pot
6119 Odana Road
Madison 53719
(608) 271-7979

Gourmet foods, Godiva chocolate, cookware, baskets, cookbooks.

Tellus Mater
409 State Street
Madison 53703
(608) 255-7027

Contemporary glassware, china, cookware, baskets, linens.

Directory of Catalogues

The catalogues listed here specialize in tableware and kitchenware. Their merchandise is la crème de la crème in terms of style, quality, and reliability.

Cherchez
864 Lexington Avenue
New York, New York 10021
(212) 737-8215

Potpourri, fine linens, antique lace, porcelain.

Crate and Barrel
190 Northfield Road
Northfield, Illinois 60093
(312) 446-9300

Contemporary cookware, glassware, tableware, housewares.

Descamps
723 Madison Avenue
New York, New York 10021
(212) 355-2522

Imported French table linens.

Gump's
250 Post Street
San Francisco, California 94108
(800) 227-4512

Excellent selection of china, crystal, flatware; specializing in Oriental antiques.

H. Roth & Son
1577 First Avenue
New York, New York 10028
(212) 734-1110

Baskets, cookware, cookbooks, kitchenware, herbs, foods, coffees and teas.

The Horchow Collection
4435 Simonton Road
Dallas, Texas 75234
(800) 527-0303

Always changing assortment of objects for the table and home.

James Robinson, Inc.
15 East 57th Street
New York, New York 10022
(212) 752-6166

Handmade sterling flatware and tea and coffee services; fine antique silver, porcelain, glass.

Laura Ashley, Inc.
714 Madison Avenue
New York, New York 10021
(212) 371-0099

English country prints on china, crockery, napkins, place mats, and fabric.

Quimper Faience
141 Water Street
Stonington, Connecticut 06378
(203) 535-1712

Devoted exclusively to the French provincial hand-painted earthenware of Quimper, France.

Tiffany & Co.
727 Fifth Avenue
New York, New York 10022
(800) 526-0649

In New Jersey (800) 452-9146
Fine selection of china, crystal, sterling flatware, table accessories.

The Wicker Garden
1318 Madison Avenue
New York, New York 10028
(212) 410-7000

Antique wicker tables, chairs, high chairs, trays, baskets; antique tablecloths and napkins.

Williams-Sonoma
5750 Hollis Street
Emeryville, California 94608
(415) 652-1555

International collection of tableware, kitchenware, and specialty foods.

Wolfman·Gold & Good Company
484 Broome Street
New York, New York 10013
(212) 431-1888

Extensive selection of oversized white dinnerware and glassware; French bistro flatware, fine French linens, antique linens and flatware; baskets; large selection of specially imported French paper doilies.

Zabar's
2245 Broadway
New York, New York 10024
(212) 787-2000

Gourmet foods, cookware, and kitchenware.

Acknowledgments

For us, the publication of *The Perfect Setting* is a dream come true. But it could never have been possible without the enthusiasm, energy, and talents of our friends who so generously worked with us.

• To our special friends, who gave their time and moral support from beginning to end, many thanks; in particular, to Janet Kramer whose help and encouragement went into writing this book. And to Pat Sadowsky, who knows where to find everything and is willing to tell; to John Uher, who assisted in the photography throughout and never lost his sense of humor; to Deanna Littell, Mary Emmerling, Suzanne Slesin, Judy Cook, Elizabeth Eakins, Bob Ciano, Paula Glatzer, Joe Toto, and David Parker.

• To all of the people who invited us into their homes and to their tables: Carlene and Ed Safdie, in whose country house we spent lovely weekends and photographed beautiful settings, Mary and Edward Higgins, Lynn and David Kaufelt, Dara and Mark Perlbinder, Penny and Charlie Peet, and, of course, everyone whose tables are sprinkled throughout these pages.

• To all the people who gave us the freedom to work on this book: Tom Grimes, who was the calm in the middle of chaos and impossible to do without; Sharron Lewis, who ran Wolfman · Gold & Good Company with unparalleled good humor and energy; Pearl Jenkins, always cheerful and always ready to press yet another tablecloth; and Phyllis Gilbert, who kept our home in order.

• To Tracy, Lucy, Betsy, Kathy, Earl, and everyone at Wolfman · Gold who ran so many extra errands for us.

• To all the people who loaned us special things and gave us invaluable information: Susan Friedman of Clarence House; Edward Munves of James Robinson; Paul Lerner of Jacques Jugeat; Lee Bailey of Bendel's; Diane Fisher and Stanley Platos of Tablescapes; Lee Stout of Knoll International; Joel Dean, Giorgio DeLuca, and Jack Ceglic of Dean & DeLuca; Patrizia Anichini and Susan Dollenmaier, who loaned us their beautiful antique linens; Judi Boisson, who let us choose from her exceptional collection of American quilts; and Shirley Cohen, our partner in Doily Carte, who helped us collect our directory of stores.

• To our friend Polly Talbott, who helped us test and develop recipes; to Andrea Dean, who so artistically arranged the basket of summer crudités and other beauties.

• To Naomi Warner, who opened the doors at Abrams for us, thank you.

• To the special people at Abrams who took such a personal interest in our book: Margaret Kaplan, Sam Antupit, Judith Tortolano, Judith Henry, and our editor Ruth Peltason, a most welcome new friend.

• To our boys Erik, Benjamin, Alexander, and Jeremy, who willingly tasted all of our recipes, but never quite learned the art of clearing the table.

PERI WOLFMAN & CHARLEY GOLD

MORNING SETTINGS

*B*reakfast can be as cheerful and lively as cornflakes with the kids, as sensually indulgent as breakfast in bed, as extravagantly stylish as a champagne brunch. During the week, the morning meal is a great setting for a business discussion, a committee meeting, a gossip with an old friend before the telephone rings and the day starts in earnest. But on weekends and on vacations, the morning meal becomes an occasion.

Morning settings are endlessly adaptable, not only to one's psyche but also to the season and the weather. A cold and snowy morning calls for a substantial meal served in a warm and cozy setting; a sunny summer day suggests light fruit eaten out-of-doors.

Breakfast foods are inherently beautiful, and one needs only to look to the food itself for decorative inspiration. Voluptuous muffins, crusty breads, a vivid rainbow of jellies, glass pitchers glistening with juice—such foods preclude the need for additional embellishment. Things of a kind make strikingly handsome compositions, whether it's a bowl heaped with eggs, a footed compote stacked with lemons, or a basket of oranges.

Especially important for the morning, when time is of the essence, is keeping staples stored in containers that can go from refrigerator or cupboard right to the table. Jars of jam are kept in a basket in the refrigerator, butter in a porcelain crock, sugar in anything that strikes your fancy. We decant and remove from cartons our potables as soon as they come from the store.

Most of us approach breakfast with minimal expectations. Therefore, when it is beautifully, thoughtfully, artfully presented, it is a very special treat, indeed.*

Hereafter, an asterisk appearing at the end of a description connotes a recipe provided in the recipe chapter.